Mac OS® X
v.10.4 Tiger™

maranGraphics™

&

THOMSON
━━━━━━━━━━━━━━━ ™
COURSE TECHNOLOGY

Professional ■ Technical ■ Reference

MARAN ILLUSTRATED™ Mac OS® X v.10.4 Tiger™

Distributed in the U.S. and Canada by Thomson Course Technology PTR. For enquiries about Maran Illustrated™ books outside the U.S. and Canada, please contact maranGraphics at international@maran.com

For U.S. orders and customer service, please contact Thomson Course Technology at 1-800-354-9706. For Canadian orders, please contact Thomson Course Technology at 1-800-268-2222 or 416-752-9448.

ISBN: 1-59200-878-X

Library of Congress Catalog Card Number: 2005921019

Printed in the United States of America

05 06 07 08 09 BU 10 9 8 7 6 5 4 3

Trademarks

Permissions

Apple
Screen shots reprinted by permission from Apple Computer, Inc.

CBS SportsLine
Copyright © 2005 SportsLine USA, Inc. http://www.sportsline.com All rights reserved.

Discovery Channel Online
Screen shots reprinted by permission from Discovery Channel Online.

Google
Screen shots reprinted by permission from Google.

Milk Web Site
Screen shots reprinted by permission from the Milk web site.

Smithsonian Institution
Copyright © 2005 Smithsonian Institution.

Sunkist
Screen shots reprinted by permission from Sunkist.

Wal-Mart
Copyright © 2005 Wal-Mart Stores, Inc.

YAHOO!
Text and artwork copyright © 2005 by Yahoo! Inc. All rights reserved. YAHOO! and the YAHOO! logo are trademarks of YAHOO!, Inc.

Important

Copies

maranGraphics®

maranGraphics Inc.
5755 Coopers Avenue
Mississauga, Ontario
L4Z 1R9
www.maran.com

THOMSON

COURSE TECHNOLOGY™
Professional ■ Technical ■ Reference

Thomson Course Technology PTR, a division of Thomson Course Technology
25 Thomson Place ■ Boston, MA 02210 ■ http://www.courseptr.com

maranGraphics is a family-run business.

At **maranGraphics**, we believe in producing great computer books– one book at a time.

Each maranGraphics book uses the award-winning communication process that we have been developing over the last 30 years. Using this process, we organize screen shots and text in a way that makes it easy for you to learn new concepts and tasks.

We spend hours deciding the best way to perform each task, so you don't have to! Our clear, easy-to-follow screen shots and instructions walk you through each task from beginning to end.

We want to thank you for purchasing what we feel are the best books money can buy. We hope you enjoy using this book as much as we enjoyed creating it!

Sincerely,

The Maran Family

We would love to hear from you! Send your comments and feedback about our books to family@maran.com

Please visit us on the Web at:
www.maran.com

Credits

Authors:
Ruth Maran
Kelleigh Johnson

Technical Consultant & Post Production:
Robert Maran

Project Manager & Editor:
Judy Maran

Editor:
Jill Maran Dutfield

Layout Artist & Illustrator:
Richard Hung

Illustrators:
Russ Marini
Sarah Kim

Indexer:
Kelleigh Johnson

President, Thomson Course Technology:
David R. West

Senior Vice President of Business Development, Thomson Course Technology:
Andy Shafran

Publisher and General Manager, Thomson Course Technology PTR:
Stacy L. Hiquet

Associate Director of Marketing, Thomson Course Technology PTR:
Sarah O'Donnell

National Sales Manager, Thomson Course Technology PTR:
Amy Merrill

Manager of Editorial Services, Thomson Course Technology PTR:
Heather Talbot

Acknowledgments

Thanks to the dedicated staff of maranGraphics, including Richard Hung, Kelleigh Johnson, Sarah Kim, Jill Maran, Judy Maran, Robert Maran, Ruth Maran, Russ Marini and Andrew Wheeler.

Finally, to Richard Maran who originated the easy-to-use graphic format of this guide. Thank you for your inspiration and guidance.

TABLE OF CONTENTS

Chapter 1

MAC OS X BASICS

Chapter 2

VIEW FILES

Chapter 3

WORK WITH FILES

Chapter 4

CUSTOMIZE YOUR COMPUTER

TABLE OF CONTENTS

Chapter 5

USING MAC OS X APPLICATIONS

Chapter 6

WORK WITH SONGS AND VIDEOS

Chapter 7

MANAGE PHOTOS

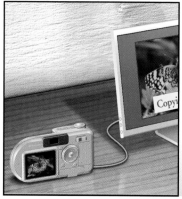

Chapter 8

CREATE MOVIES

Chapter 9

SHARE YOUR COMPUTER

TABLE OF CONTENTS

Chapter 10

WORK ON A NETWORK

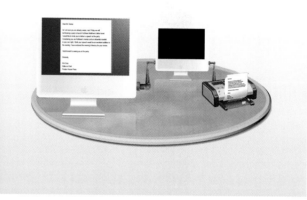

Chapter 11

BROWSE THE WEB

Chapter 12

Chapter 13

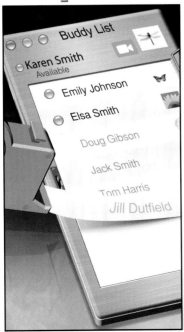

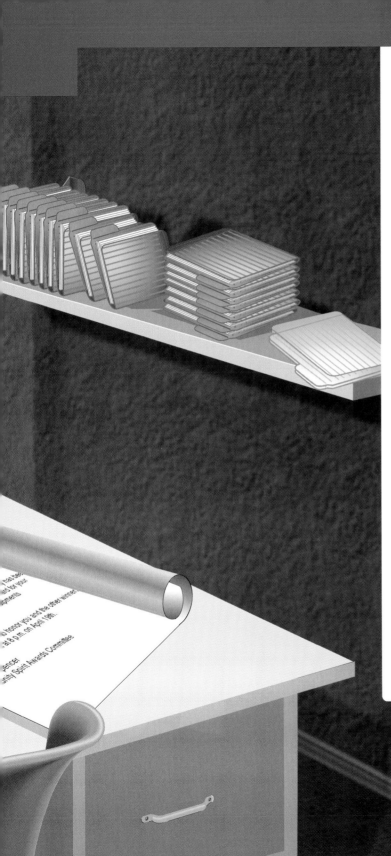

CHAPTER 1

Mac OS X Basics

In this chapter, you will learn everything you need to know to get started using Mac OS X. Find out how to navigate the Dock, move and resize windows, close an application that is not responding, and more.

INTRODUCTION TO MAC OS X

Mac OS® X v. 10.4 Tiger Edition controls the overall activity of your computer and ensures that all parts of your computer work together smoothly and efficiently.

Work with Files

Mac OS X allows you to effectively manage the files stored on your computer. You can open, rename, duplicate, move, delete, print and search for files. You can also copy files to a recordable CD or DVD.

Customize Mac OS X

You can customize Mac OS X to suit your preferences. You can change the picture used to decorate your desktop, change the way your mouse works and turn on speech recognition to use spoken commands to perform tasks on your computer. Mac OS X also allows you to change the screen saver that appears when you do not use your computer for a period of time.

Use Mac OS X Applications

Mac OS X offers many applications you can use to perform tasks on your computer. You can use TextEdit to create documents, Address Book to store information for people you frequently contact and Font Book to view and manage fonts on your computer. You can also use Dashboard to quickly access mini-applications on your desktop.

Work With Music and Videos

Mac OS X allows you to play music CDs, create playlists that contain your favorite songs, create your own music CDs and copy songs from your computer to an iPod. You can also watch QuickTime and DVD movies on your computer.

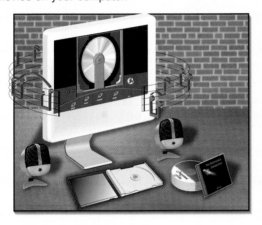

Manage Photos and Create Movies

You can use iPhoto to copy photos from a digital camera to your computer so you can view, organize and edit the photos. You can use iMovie HD to transfer video from a camcorder to your computer so you can organize and edit the video before sharing it with friends and family.

Share Your Computer

If you share your computer with other people, you can create a separate user account for each person to keep the personal files and settings for each person separate. You can also share files with other users, quickly switch between users without having to quit your applications and set parental controls for younger users.

Access the Internet

Mac OS X offers several applications you can use to access the Internet. Safari™ allows you to browse through information on the Web. You can use Mail to exchange electronic mail and iChat to exchange instant messages with friends and family over the Internet.

USING THE DOCK

The Dock appears at the bottom of your screen and allows you to quickly access the most commonly used applications.

The Dock automatically displays icons for several applications, such as Mail, Address Book, iCal and System Preferences.

USING THE DOCK

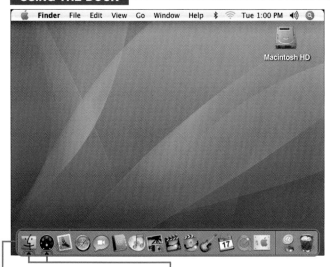

■ By default, the Dock appears at the bottom of your screen and displays the icons for several applications.

■ A triangle (▲) appears below the icon for each application that is currently open.

<u>IDENTIFY A DOCK ICON</u>

1 To identify an icon in the Dock, position the mouse ▶ over the icon.

■ The name of the icon appears above the Dock.

Will other icons appear in the Dock as I work?

When you open an application that does not appear in the Dock by default, an icon for the application appears to the left of the line in the Dock. The icon for the application will disappear when you quit the application.

When you minimize a window, an icon for the window appears to the right of the line in the Dock. To minimize a window, see page 26.

**Open
Application**   **Minimized
Window**

Can I use the Dock to quickly quit an application?

Yes. Press and hold down the `control` key as you click the icon for the application you want to quit. On the menu that appears, click **Quit** to quit the application.

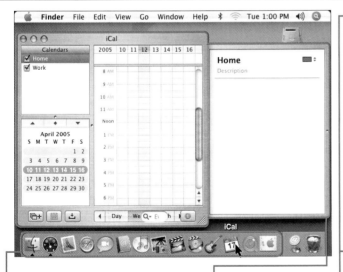

OPEN AN APPLICATION

1 To open an application displayed in the Dock, click the icon for the application.

■ When you open an application, the application's icon bounces while the application opens.

■ The application appears on your screen.

QUIT AN APPLICATION

1 When you finish working with an application, click the icon for the application in the Dock.

■ This area displays the menu bar for the application you selected.

2 Click the name of the application in the menu bar.

3 Click **Quit** to quit the application.

Note: You cannot quit the Finder or Dashboard applications.

17

SCROLL THROUGH A WINDOW

You can use a scroll bar to browse through the information in a window. Scrolling is useful when a window is not large enough to display all the information in the window.

SCROLL THROUGH A WINDOW

SCROLL UP OR DOWN

1 Click ▲ or ▼ to scroll up or down through the information in a window.

Note: If all the information in a window is displayed, you cannot scroll through the window.

SCROLL TO ANY POSITION

1 Position the mouse ▸ over the scroller on a scroll bar.

2 Drag the scroller along the scroll bar until the information you want to view appears.

■ The location of the scroller indicates which part of the window you are viewing. For example, when the scroller is halfway down the scroll bar, you are viewing information from the middle of the window.

CLOSE A WINDOW

When you finish
working with a
window, you can
close the window
to remove it from
your screen.

CLOSE A WINDOW

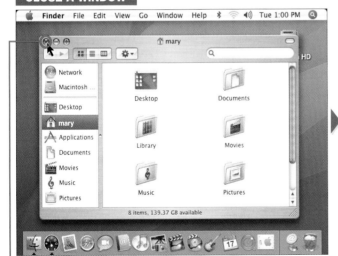

1 Click ⊙ in the window
you want to close.

■ The window disappears
from your screen.

*Note: To close all windows in the
same application at once, such
as all your open word processing
files, press and hold down the*
option *key as you click* ⊙ *in
one of the application's windows.*

USING THE SIDEBAR

Finder windows display a Sidebar that allows you to quickly access commonly used disks and folders on your computer.

You can hide the Sidebar at any time to reduce clutter in a window and display more of the window's contents. You can also add a file or folder you frequently access to the Sidebar. The item you add will appear in the Sidebar of all your Finder windows.

USING THE SIDEBAR

1 To display the contents of a Sidebar location in a window, click the location in the Sidebar.

■ The contents of the location appear in the window.

HIDE THE SIDEBAR

1 To hide the Sidebar in a Finder window, click ⬭ in the window.

Note: If the ⬭ button is not available in a window, you cannot hide the Sidebar.

■ The Sidebar disappears from the window.

Note: The tool area at the top of the window also disappears.

■ To once again display the Sidebar and tool area in the window, click ⬭ .

Tip

What locations are available in the Sidebar?

Location:	Displays Contents of:
Network	The Network window. See page 242.
Macintosh HD	Your hard disk. See page 36.
Desktop	Your desktop.
Your User Name	Your home folder. See page 34.
Applications	The Applications folder.
Documents	Your Documents folder.
Movies	Your Movies folder.
Music	Your Music folder.
Pictures	Your Pictures folder.

Tip

How can I remove a location I no longer need from the Sidebar?

If the Sidebar displays items you do not frequently use, you can remove the items to reduce the clutter in the Sidebar. To remove an item from the Sidebar, position the mouse ▶ over the item you want to remove and then drag the item out of the Sidebar. The item disappears in a puff of smoke. Removing an item from the sidebar does not remove the item from your computer.

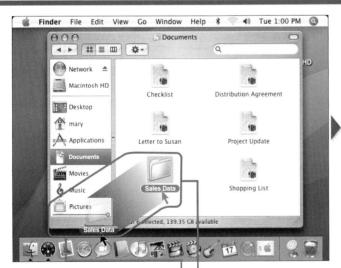

ADD AN ITEM TO THE SIDEBAR

1 To add a file or folder you frequently access to the Sidebar that appears in Finder windows, open a Finder window on your desktop.

2 Position the mouse ▶ over the file or folder you want to add to the Sidebar.

3 Drag the file or folder to the bottom of the Sidebar.

Note: A blue line indicates where the item will appear.

■ The name of the file or folder appears in the Sidebar. You can now click the file or folder in the Sidebar to display the contents of the file or folder.

Note: A file or folder you add to the Sidebar will be available in the Sidebar of every Finder window you open.

SWITCH BETWEEN WINDOWS

If you have more than one window open on your screen, you can easily switch between the windows.

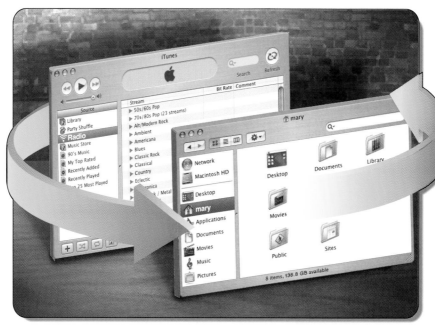

Each window is like a separate piece of paper. Switching between windows is like placing a different piece of paper at the top of the pile.

SWITCH BETWEEN WINDOWS

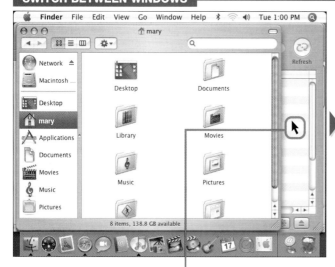

■ You can work in only one window at a time. The active window appears in front of all other windows.

1 Click inside a window you want to make the active window.

■ The window becomes active and appears in front of all the other windows. You can now clearly view the contents of the window.

■ This area displays the menu bar for the active window.

Note: The menu bar changes, depending on the active window. Make sure the window you want to work with is the active window before using the menu bar to perform a task.

Tip

Can I quickly clear all open windows from my screen so I can access the desktop?

Yes. Mac OS X allows you to instantly remove all the windows from your screen. Press the F11 key to hide all your open windows so you can view and work with items on the desktop. To once again display all open windows on the desktop, press the F11 key again.

Tip

Is there another way I can make an application window the active window?

If an icon for the application you want to work with appears in the Dock, you can click the icon in the Dock to make the application window the active window. The application window will move in front of all the other open windows.

QUICKLY VIEW ALL OPEN WINDOWS

■ If you cannot click inside the window you want to make the active window, you can have Mac OS X arrange the open windows for you.

1 Press the F9 key to reduce the size of all the open windows and arrange them on your screen.

■ Each open window is displayed on your desktop so you can view all the windows at once.

2 Move the mouse 🖑 over a window of interest.

■ The name of the window appears in the center of the window.

3 To make a window the active window, click the window.

■ All your open windows return to normal size and the active window appears in front of all the other windows.

MOVE A WINDOW

If a window covers items on your screen, you can move the window to a different location on the screen.

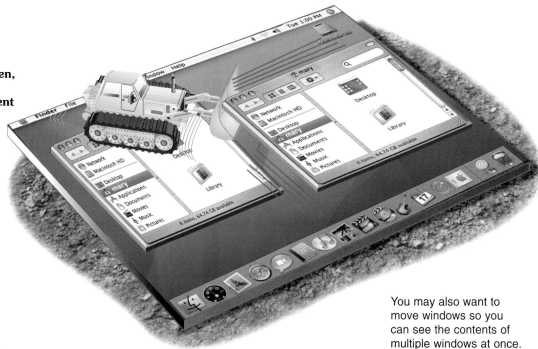

You may also want to move windows so you can see the contents of multiple windows at once.

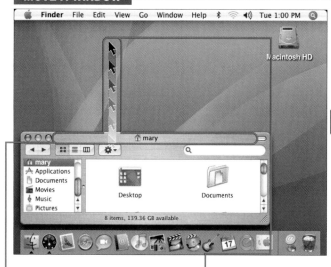

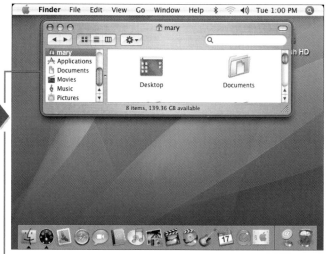

1 Position the mouse ▶ over the title bar of the window you want to move.

2 Drag the mouse ▶ to where you want to place the window.

■ The window moves to the new location.

You can easily change
the size of a window
displayed on your
screen.

Increasing the size of a
window allows you to
view more information in
the window. Decreasing
the size of a window
allows you to view items
covered by the window.

RESIZE A WINDOW

1 Position the mouse ➤
over ▨ at the bottom
right corner of the window
you want to resize.

2 Drag the mouse ➤
until the window displays
the size you want.

■ The window displays
the new size.

ZOOM A WINDOW

1 To quickly increase
or decrease the size of a
window to better display
its contents, click ⬤.

■ To return the window
to its previous size, click ⬤
again.

MINIMIZE A WINDOW

If you are not using a window, you can minimize the window to temporarily remove it from your screen. You can redisplay the window at any time.

Minimizing a window allows you to temporarily put the window aside so you can work on other tasks.

MINIMIZE A WINDOW

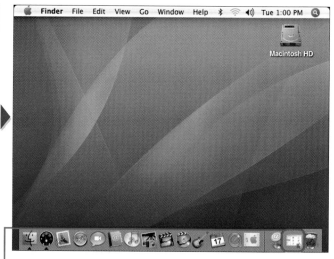

1 Click ◯ in the window you want to minimize.

■ You can also double-click the title bar of a window to minimize the window.

■ The window reduces to an icon in the Dock.

■ To redisplay the window, click its icon in the Dock.

Note: To minimize all windows in the same application at once, such as all your open word processing files, press and hold down the option *key as you click ◯ in one of the application's windows.*

If an application is no longer responding, you can force the application to quit without having to shut down your computer.

When you force an application to quit, you will lose any information you did not save in the application.

Forcing an application to quit should not affect other open applications.

FORCE AN APPLICATION TO QUIT

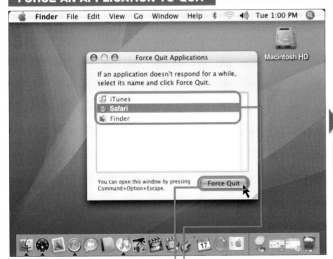

1 To force an application to quit, press and hold down the `option` and `⌘` keys as you press the `esc` key.

■ The Force Quit Applications window appears.

■ This area lists the applications that are currently open.

2 Click the application you want to quit.

3 Click **Force Quit**.

■ A dialog sheet appears, confirming that you want to quit the application.

4 Click **Force Quit** to quit the application.

5 Click ⭕ to close the Force Quit Applications window.

Note: Try restarting the application and your computer. If you continue to have problems with the application, try re-installing the application or contact the application's manufacturer for help.

27

RESTART YOUR COMPUTER

If your computer is not operating properly, you can restart the computer to try to fix the problem.

Restarting your computer shuts down the computer and then immediately starts it again.

RESTART YOUR COMPUTER

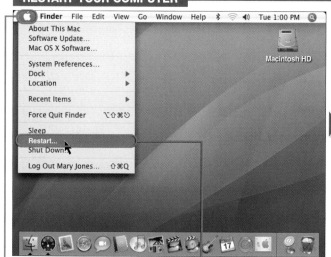

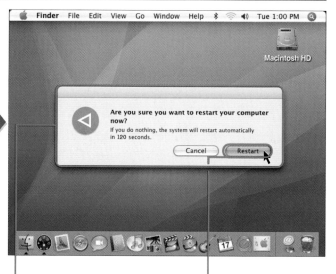

■ Before restarting your computer, make sure you close any files and applications you have open.

1 Click to display the Apple menu.

2 Click **Restart**.

■ A dialog box appears, confirming that you want to restart your computer.

3 Click **Restart** to restart your computer.

Note: If you do not perform step 3 within 2 minutes, your computer will restart automatically.

SHUT DOWN YOUR COMPUTER

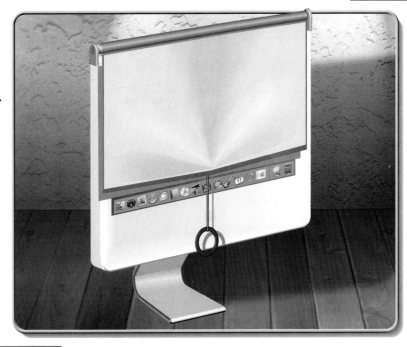

When you finish using
your computer, you
should shut down the
computer to turn it off.

If you turn off the
power to your
computer without
first shutting down
the computer, you
could lose data.

SHUT DOWN YOUR COMPUTER

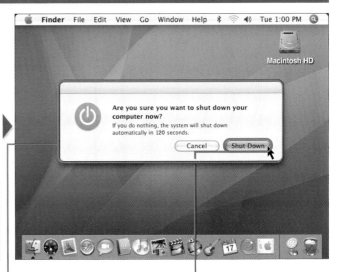

■ Before shutting down
your computer, make sure
you close any files and
applications you have open.

1 Click to display the
Apple menu.

2 Click **Shut Down**.

■ A dialog box appears,
confirming that you want to
shut down your computer.

3 Click **Shut Down** to
shut down your computer.

*Note: If you do not perform step **3**
within 2 minutes, your computer
will shut down automatically.*

GETTING HELP

If you do not know how to perform a task on your computer, you can search for help information on the task.

GETTING HELP

1 Click **Help**.

2 Click the Help command.

Note: The name of the Help command depends on the active application.

■ The Help window appears.

■ This area may display links to information about the active application. You can click a link to browse through the available information.

3 To search for specific help information about a topic, click this area and type a word or phrase that describes the topic of interest.

4 To start the search, press the `return` key.

Tip

Why does blue text appear at the bottom of some help pages?

Some help pages display blue text that you can click to obtain additional help. A bold, black heading often appears above the blue text to indicate how the blue text can help you. For example, clicking blue text below the **See also** heading will display a related help topic. Clicking blue text below the **Open this for me** heading opens a window, application or Web page for you.

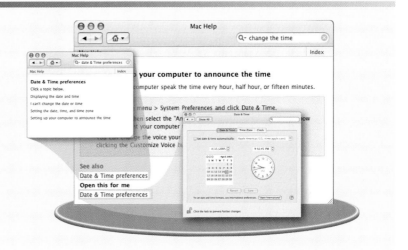

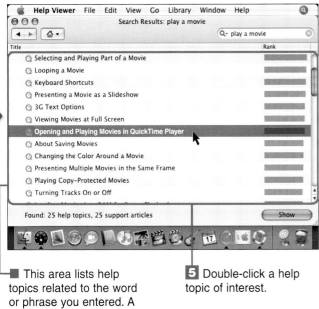

■ This area lists help topics related to the word or phrase you entered. A bar beside each help topic indicates the relevance of the topic to the word or phrase you entered.

5 Double-click a help topic of interest.

■ The information for the help topic you selected appears.

■ You can click ◄ or ► to move backward or forward through the help pages you have viewed.

Note: The ► button is available only after you use the ◄ button to return to a previous help page.

6 When you finish reviewing help information, click ⬤ to close the Help window.

CHAPTER 2

View Files

Read this chapter to learn how to view the files and folders stored on your computer as well as the contents of a CD or DVD.

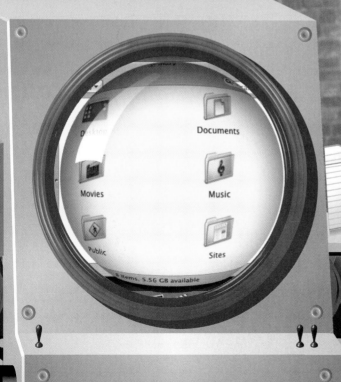

VIEW

VIEW PERSONAL FOLDERS AND APPLICATIONS

You can view the personal folders and applications stored on your computer.

The home folder stores your personal folders, which provide a convenient place for you to store and manage your files.

The Applications folder stores the applications available on your computer. Mac OS X comes with many applications that you can use.

VIEW PERSONAL FOLDERS

1 Click **Go**.

Note: If Go is not available, click a blank area on your desktop to display the Finder menu bar.

2 Click **Home** to view your personal folders.

■ A window appears, displaying your personal folders.

■ To display the contents of a personal folder, double-click the folder.

■ You can also click your name in any open window to view your personal folders.

3 When you finish viewing your personal folders, click ⬤ to close the window.

Tip

What personal folders does Tiger include?

Desktop Stores the items displayed on the desktop.		**Movies, Music and Pictures** Provide convenient places to store your movies, music and pictures.	
Documents Provides a convenient place to store files you create.		**Public** Stores files you want to share with every user on your computer. For more information on the Public folder, see page 235.	
Library Stores items such as fonts and sounds for your user account.		**Sites** Stores Web pages you create that you want to make available on the Internet.	

VIEW APPLICATIONS

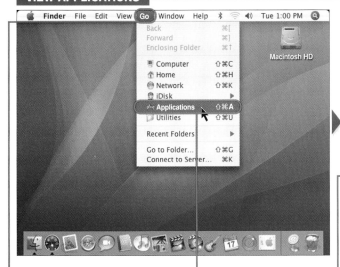

1 Click **Go**.

Note: If Go is not available, click a blank area on your desktop to display the Finder menu bar.

2 Click **Applications** to view the applications available on your computer.

■ The Applications window appears, displaying the applications available on your computer.

■ To start an application, double-click the application.

■ You can also click **Applications** in any open window to view the applications available on your computer.

3 When you finish viewing the applications available on your computer, click ○ to close the Applications window.

VIEW THE CONTENTS OF YOUR COMPUTER

You can easily browse through the disks, folders and files on your computer.

Like a filing cabinet, Mac OS X uses folders to organize the files, such as documents, pictures, sounds and videos, stored on your computer.

VIEW THE CONTENTS OF YOUR COMPUTER

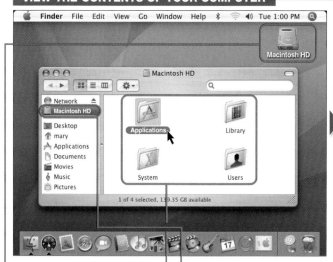

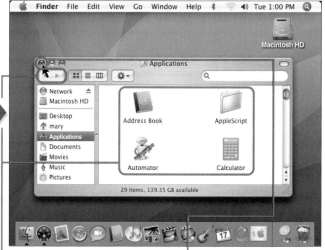

VIEW THE CONTENTS OF YOUR HARD DISK

1 Double-click the hard disk icon on the desktop to view the contents of your hard disk.

■ A window appears, displaying the contents of your hard disk.

■ You can also click the name of the hard disk in any open window to display the contents of the hard disk.

2 To display the contents of a folder, double-click the folder.

■ The contents of the folder you selected appear.

■ To display the contents of another folder, double-click the folder.

■ You can click ◀ or ▶ to move backward or forward through the windows you have viewed.

Note: The ▶ button is available only after you click the ◀ button.

3 When you finish viewing the contents of your hard disk, click ⬤ to close the window.

Tip

What are some of the folders that Mac OS X automatically includes on my hard disk?

Applications

Stores the applications available on your computer, such as Safari and TextEdit.

Library

Stores system items available to every user account on your computer, such as desktop pictures, fonts and screen savers.

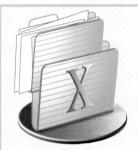

System

Stores a Library folder that contains the files Mac OS X requires to run.

Users

Stores a home folder for each user account on your computer. For more information on the Users folder, see page 234.

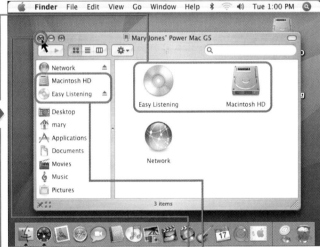

VIEW THE CONTENTS OF YOUR COMPUTER

1 Click **Go**.

Note: If Go is not available, click a blank area on your desktop to display the Finder menu bar.

2 Click **Computer** to view the disks available on your computer.

Note: The desktop also displays the disks available on your computer.

■ A window appears, displaying an icon for each disk available on your computer, including your hard disk and any CD or DVD inserted into a drive on your computer.

■ To display the contents of a disk, double-click the disk.

■ You can also click a disk in this area in any open window to display the contents of the disk.

3 When you finish viewing the contents of your computer, click ⬤ to close the window.

VIEW THE CONTENTS OF A DISC

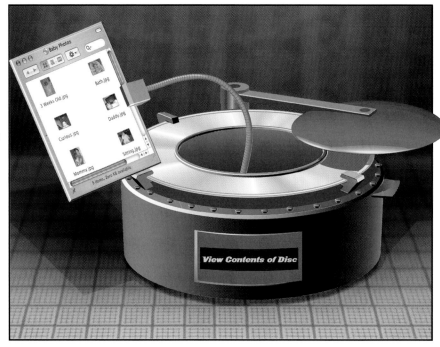

You can view the contents of a CD or DVD. When you finish working with a disc, you can eject the disc from your computer.

The drive(s) available on your computer determine what types of discs you can view.

VIEW THE CONTENTS OF A DISC

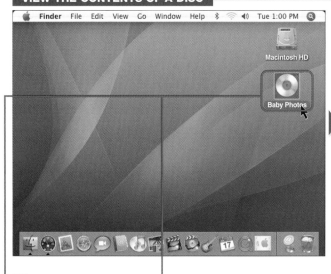

1 Insert a CD or DVD into your computer's drive.

■ An icon for the disc appears on your desktop.

Note: If the disc contains photos or music, iPhoto or iTunes may open. For information on iPhoto, see pages 176 to 193. For information on iTunes, see pages 154 to 173.

2 Double-click the disc's icon to view the contents of the disc.

■ A window appears, displaying the contents of the disc.

3 When you finish viewing the contents of the disc, click ⬤ to close the window.

Why did my computer's drive eject my disc?

Your computer's drive may eject a disc if there is a problem with the disc. For example, you may need to clean the disc or the disc may be unreadable due to scratches.

Why did a dialog box appear when I tried to eject a disc?

A dialog box may appear if one or more files on the disc are open when you try to eject the disc. To close the dialog box, click **OK**. Close the files that are open and quit any applications that may be using files on the disc. Then try to eject the disc again.

EJECT A DISC

1 To eject a disc, position the mouse ▶ over the disc's icon on your desktop.

2 Drag the disc's icon to the Trash icon (🗑 changes to ⏏).

■ The disc's icon disappears from your desktop and the disc is physically ejected from the drive.

Note: If your keyboard has an Eject key, you can also press the Eject key to eject the disc.

CHANGE THE VIEW OF ITEMS IN A WINDOW

You can change the view of items in a window. The view you select determines the way files and folders will appear in the window.

CHANGE THE VIEW OF ITEMS IN A WINDOW

1 Click a button to specify the way you want to view items in the window.

▤▤ Icons

☰ List

▥ Columns

ICONS

■ The Icons view displays items as icons.

■ By default, the name of each item appears below each icon.

Tip

Can I sort items displayed in the List view?

Yes. You can sort items by name, date last modified, size or kind. Click the heading for the column you want to use to sort the items. To sort the items in the reverse order, you can click the heading again.

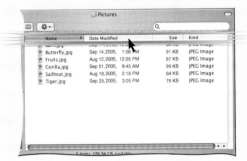

Tip

How do I change the width of a column in the List view?

To change the width of a column in the List view, position the mouse $\blacktriangle$ over the right edge of the column heading ($\blacktriangle$ changes to $\leftrightarrow$) and then drag the column edge until the column displays the width you want.

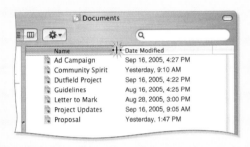

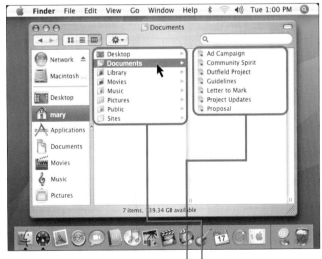

LIST

■ The List view displays items as small icons arranged in a list. This view displays information about each item, including the name, date last modified, size and kind of item.

1 To display the contents of a folder, click ▶ beside the folder (▶ changes to ▼).

■ The contents of the folder appear.

Note: To once again hide the contents of a folder, click ▼ beside the folder.

COLUMNS

■ The Columns view shows the location of the current folder in relation to the disks, folders and files on your computer.

Note: Each column shows the contents of the item selected in the previous column.

1 To display the contents of a folder, click the folder.

■ The contents of the folder appear in the next column.

SORT ITEMS

You can sort the items displayed in a window to help you find files and folders more quickly.

You can sort items by name, size, kind, date the items were last changed or created or by label color. For information on labeling files, see page 53.

SORT ITEMS

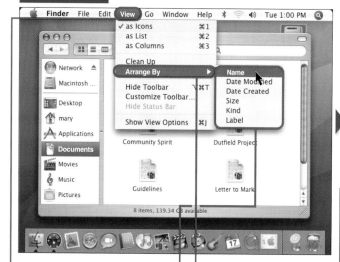

1 Click a blank area in the window that contains the items you want to sort.

Note: To sort the items on your desktop, click a blank area on the desktop.

2 Click **View**.

3 Position the mouse ▶ over **Arrange By**.

4 Click the way you want to sort the items in the window.

Note: The Arrange By command is available only when files are displayed as icons. To change the view of files, see page 40.

■ The items appear in the new order. In this example, the items are sorted by name.

You can clean up
a window by neatly
arranging the files
and folders in the
window.

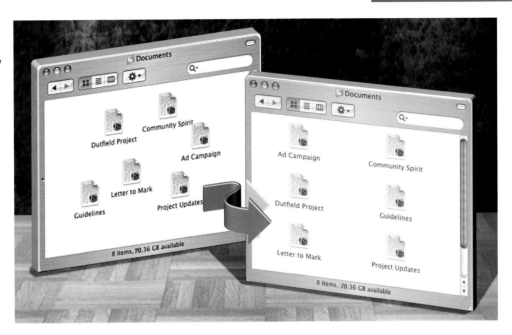

CLEAN UP A WINDOW

1 Click a blank area in
the window you want to
clean up.

*Note: To clean up the icons on
your desktop, click a blank area
on the desktop.*

2 Click **View**.

3 Click **Clean Up**.

*Note: The Clean Up command
is available only when files are
displayed as icons. To change
the view of files, see page 40.*

■ The icons move to the
nearest empty positions in
the window's invisible grid.

DISPLAY FILE INFORMATION

You can display information about a file, such as the file size and date you last modified the file.

You can display information about folders, disks, applications and aliases the same way you display information about files.

DISPLAY FILE INFORMATION

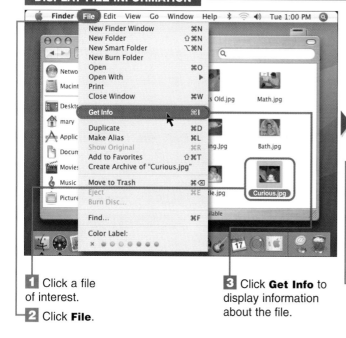

1 Click a file of interest.

2 Click **File**.

3 Click **Get Info** to display information about the file.

■ The Info window appears, displaying information about the file, including the file type, size, location, dates the file was created and modified and the label color.

4 To enter information about the file that may help you later find the file, click this area and type the information.

Note: For information on finding files, see page 63.

Tip

What additional categories of information can I display for a file?

More Info

Displays more information about the file, such as the last time the file was opened.

Name & Extension

Allows you to view and change the file name and extension of a file, such as Report.rtf.

Open with

Allows you to view and change the application that opens a file.

Preview

Allows you to preview some types of files, such as pictures, movies and sounds. If a preview is unavailable, a larger version of the file's icon appears.

Ownership & Permissions

Allows you to specify who owns a file and who you want to be able to access the file. This is useful if you share your computer with other people or are connected to a network.

■ This area displays additional categories of information you can display for the file.

Note: You may need to drag the scroller down to view all the additional categories.

5 To display the information in a category, click ▶ beside the category of interest (▶ changes to ▼).

■ The information in the category appears. In this example, information about the file's ownership and permissions appears.

■ To once again hide the information in the category, click ▼.

6 When you finish reviewing information about the file, click ⬤ to close the Info window.

CHAPTER 3

Work With Files

This chapter teaches you how to efficiently manage and work with your files. Learn how to rename and label your files, search for misplaced files, print and delete files, copy files to a CD or DVD and more.

SELECT FILES

Before working with files, you often need to select the files you want to work with. Selected files appear highlighted on your screen.

You can select folders the same way you select files. Selecting a folder selects all the files in the folder.

SELECT FILES

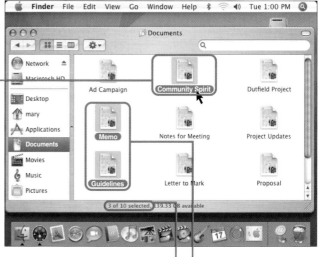

SELECT ONE FILE

1 Click the icon for the file you want to select.

■ The file is highlighted.

SELECT RANDOM FILES

1 Click the icon for a file you want to select.

2 Press and hold down the ⌘ key as you click the icon for each additional file you want to select.

■ This area displays the number of files you selected.

How can I select all the files in a window?

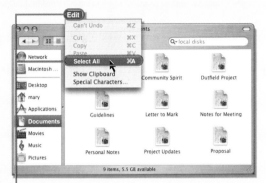

1 Click a blank area in the window that contains the files you want to select.

2 Click **Edit**.

3 Click **Select All** to select all the files in the window.

How do I deselect files?

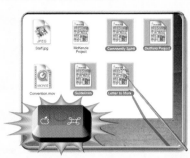

■ To deselect all the files in a window, click a blank area in the window.

■ To deselect one or more files from a group of selected files, press and hold down the ⌘ key as you click the icon for each file you want to deselect.

Note: You can deselect folders the same way you deselect files.

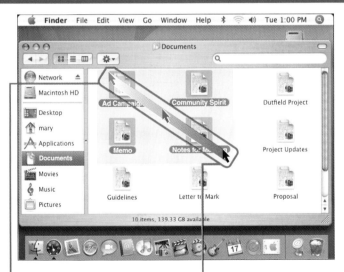

SELECT A GROUP OF FILES

1 Position the mouse slightly above and to the left of the first file you want to select.

2 Drag the mouse diagonally across the files you want to select.

■ While you drag the mouse, a box appears around the files that will be selected.

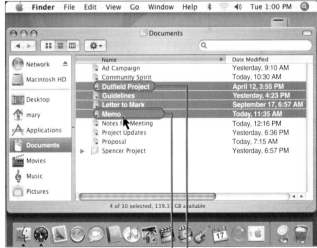

SELECT A GROUP OF FILES IN LIST OR COLUMNS VIEW

■ You can use this method to select a group of files in the List or Columns view. To change the view of files, see page 40.

1 Click the icon for the first file you want to select.

2 Press and hold down the **shift** key as you click the icon for the last file you want to select.

OPEN A FILE

You can open a file to display its contents on your screen. Opening a file allows you to review and make changes to the file.

You can open a folder the same way you open a file.

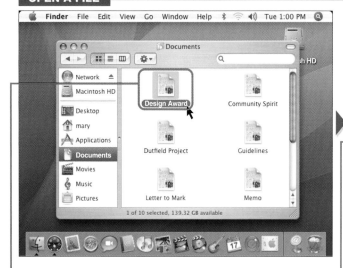

1 Double-click the icon for the file you want to open.

■ The file opens. You can review and make changes to the file.

Note: If you opened a picture, the picture opens in the Preview application. The Preview application allows you to only review the picture. For information on the Preview application, see page 68.

2 When you finish working with the file, click ⬤ to close the file.

OPEN A RECENTLY USED FILE

Mac OS X keeps track of the files you have recently used. You can quickly open any of these files.

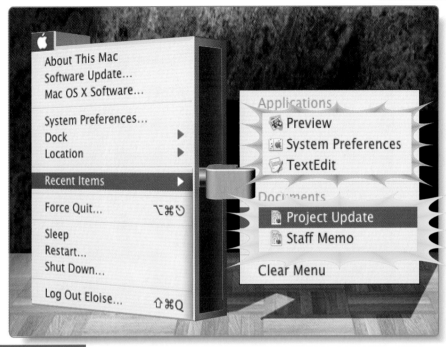

Mac OS X also keeps track of applications you have recently used. You can open a recently used application at any time.

OPEN A RECENTLY USED FILE

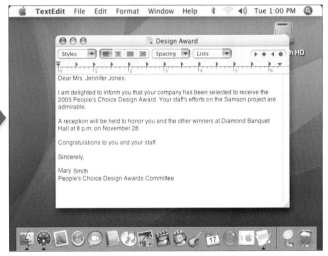

1 Click to display the Apple menu.

2 Position the mouse ▸ over **Recent Items**.

■ A list of files and applications you have recently used appears.

3 Click the file you want to open.

Note: You can click an application to open the application.

■ The file you selected opens.

*Note: To clear the list of files and applications you have recently used, perform steps 1 to 3, selecting **Clear Menu** in step 3. Clearing the list of recently used files and applications will not delete the items from your computer.*

RENAME A FILE

You can rename a file to better describe the contents of the file. Renaming a file can help you more quickly locate the file in the future.

You can rename folders the same way you rename files. You should not rename folders that Mac OS X or your applications require to operate.

RENAME A FILE

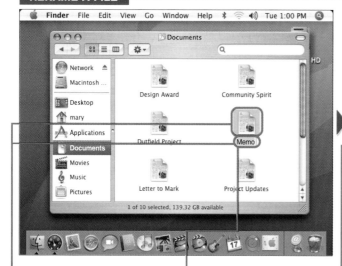

1 Click the icon for the file you want to rename to select the file.

2 Click the name of the file you selected.

■ After a moment, a box appears around the file name and the file name is selected.

Note: If a box does not appear around the file name, press the return *key.*

3 Type a new name for the file and then press the return key.

Note: A file name cannot contain a colon (:) or begin with a period (.). Each file in the same location must have a unique name.

■ If you change your mind while typing a new file name, you can press the esc key to return to the original file name.

You can add color labels to your files and folders to color code information on your computer.

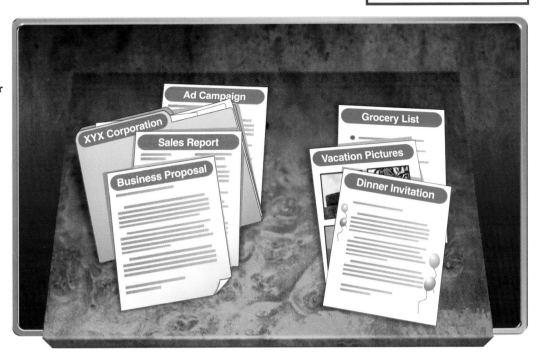

You can use color labels to help organize items on your computer. For example, business files and folders may display red color labels while personal files and folders display green color labels.

LABEL A FILE

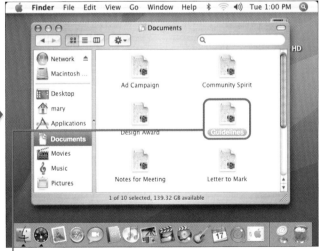

1 Click the icon for the file or folder you want to label.

2 Click **File**.

3 Click the color you want to use to label the file or folder.

■ The file name displays the color label you selected.

Note: To clearly view the color label, click outside the icon for the file or folder.

■ To remove a color label from a file or folder, perform steps **1** to **3**, except select ⊠ in step **3**.

CREATE A FOLDER

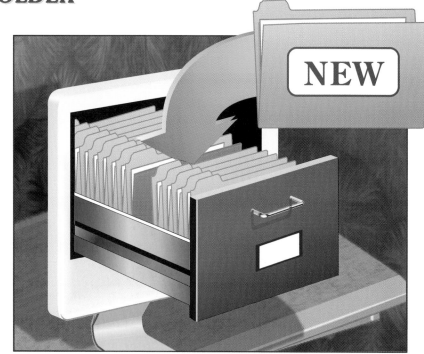

You can create a new folder to help organize the files stored on your computer.

Creating a new folder is useful when you want to keep related files together, such as the files for a particular project.

After you create a new folder, you can move files and other folders to the new folder. To move files and folders, see page 58.

CREATE A FOLDER

1 Click anywhere in the window for the folder you want to contain a new folder.

■ To create a new folder on your desktop, click a blank area on the desktop.

2 Click **File**.

3 Click **New Folder** to create a new folder.

■ The new folder appears, displaying a temporary name.

4 Type a name for the new folder and then press the [return] key.

Note: If you cannot type a name, press the [return] key and then perform step 4.

■ A folder name cannot contain a colon (:) or begin with a period (.). Each folder in the same location must have a unique name.

DELETE A FILE

You can delete a file you no longer need. The Trash stores all the files you delete.

You can delete a folder the same way you delete a file. When you delete a folder, all the files in the folder are also deleted.

Before you delete a file, make sure you will no longer need the file. You should also make sure you do not delete a file that Mac OS X or your applications require to operate.

DELETE A FILE

1 Position the mouse ▶ over the file you want to delete.

■ To delete more than one file, select all the files you want to delete. To select multiple files, see page 48.

2 Drag the file to the Trash icon.

Note: To delete a file, you can also click the icon for the file and then press and hold down the ⌘ key as you press the delete *key.*

■ The file disappears.

■ Mac OS X places the file in the Trash in case you later want to restore the file. To restore a file from the Trash, see page 56.

■ Files you delete remain in the Trash until you empty the Trash. To empty the Trash, see page 57.

RESTORE A DELETED FILE

The Trash stores all the files you have deleted. You can easily restore any file from the Trash.

You can restore folders the same way you restore files. When you restore a folder, Mac OS X restores all the files in the folder.

After deleting files, you can empty the Trash to create more free space on your computer. When you empty the Trash, the files in the Trash are removed from your computer and cannot be restored.

RESTORE A DELETED FILE

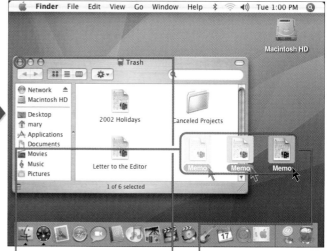

■ The appearance of the Trash icon indicates whether or not the Trash contains deleted files.

🗑 Contains deleted files.

🗑 Does not contain deleted files.

1 Click the Trash icon.

■ The Trash window appears, displaying all the files you have deleted.

2 Position the mouse ▶ over the file you want to restore.

■ To restore more than one file, select all the files you want to restore. To select multiple files, see page 48.

3 Drag the file to the desktop or to a folder.

■ The file will disappear from the Trash window and move to the location you specified.

4 Click ⬤ to close the Trash window.

Tip

How can I ensure that no one will be able to retrieve data from files I have deleted after I empty the Trash?

Even after you delete files from the Trash, it may still be possible for an experienced user to access the data that was stored in the files. Mac OS X allows you to securely delete files from the Trash. When you choose to securely empty the Trash, your computer writes random data over the deleted files to make it more difficult for other people to retrieve the original data.

■ To securely empty the Trash, perform steps 1 to 4 on page 57, except select **Secure Empty Trash** in step 3.

EMPTY THE TRASH

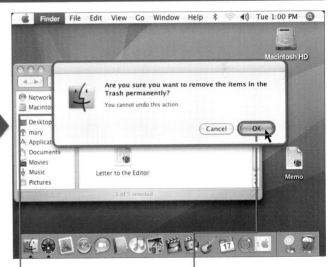

1 Click the Trash icon.

■ The Trash window appears, displaying all the files you have deleted.

2 Click **Finder**.

3 Click **Empty Trash**.

■ A warning dialog box appears, confirming that you want to permanently remove all the files in the Trash.

4 Click **OK** to permanently remove all the files in the Trash and close the Trash window.

MOVE OR COPY A FILE

You can move or copy a file to a new location on your computer.

You can move or copy a file to the desktop, a folder or another disk.

You can move or copy a folder the same way you move or copy a file. When you move or copy a folder, all the files in the folder are also moved or copied.

MOVE A FILE

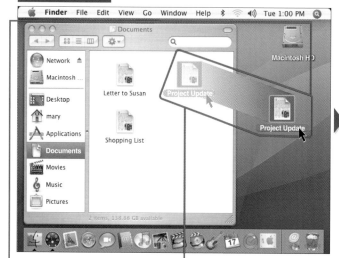

■ Before moving a file, make sure you can clearly see the location where you want to move the file.

1 Position the mouse ➤ over the file you want to move.

■ To move more than one file at once, select all the files you want to move. Then position the mouse ➤ over one of the files. To select multiple files, see page 48.

2 Drag the file to a new location.

■ The file moves to the new location.

■ The file disappears from its original location.

Tip

Can I quickly move or copy a file to a commonly used folder?

Yes. Mac OS X displays a list of commonly used disks and folders, such as Documents and Pictures, in the Sidebar of every open Finder window. You can use the methods described below to move or copy a file to one of these commonly used disks or folders. A blue highlight appears around the name of the disk or folder the file will be moved or copied to. For more information on the Sidebar, see page 20.

Tip

When I drag a file to another disk, why does Mac OS X copy rather than move the file?

When you drag a file to another disk, Mac OS X creates a copy of the file on the other disk. To move a file to another disk instead of copying the file, press and hold down the ⌘ key as you drag the file.

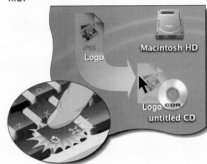

COPY A FILE

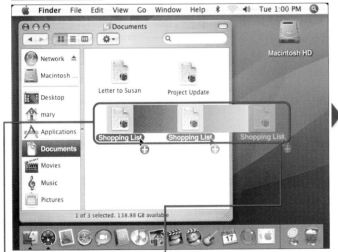

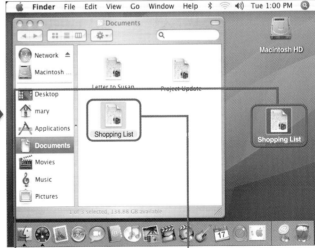

■ Before copying a file, make sure you can clearly see the location where you want to copy the file.

1 Position the mouse ▶ over the file you want to copy.

■ To copy more than one file at once, select all the files you want to copy. Then position the mouse ▶ over one of the files. To select multiple files, see page 48.

2 Press and hold down the `option` key as you drag the file to a new location.

■ A copy of the file appears in the new location.

■ The original file remains in the original location.

CREATE AN ALIAS

You can create an
alias for a file you
frequently use to
provide a quick
way of opening
the file.

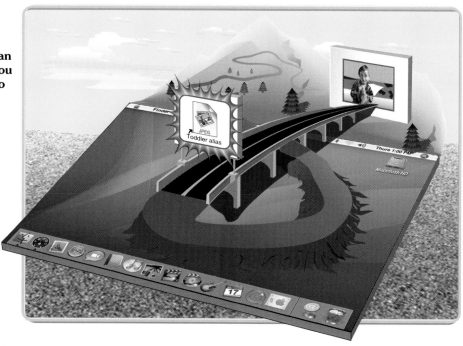

An alias points
to an original
file. If you
delete the
original file,
the alias will
no longer work.

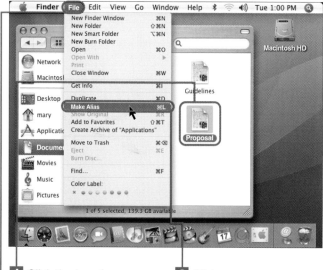

1 Click the icon for
the file you want to
create an alias for.

2 Click **File**.

3 Click **Make Alias**.

■ The alias appears,
displaying a temporary
name.

4 To use the temporary
name, press the return
key.

*Note: To use a different name,
type the new name and then
press the* return *key.*

■ You can tell the
difference between the
alias and the original
file because the alias
displays an arrow (↗).

Tip

Can I create an alias to a folder or application on my computer?

You can create an alias for a folder or an application the same way you create an alias for a file. Creating an alias for a folder gives you quick access to all the files in the folder. Creating an alias for an application allows you to quickly start the application.

Tip

How do I rename or delete an alias?

You can rename or delete an alias the same way you would rename or delete any file. Renaming or deleting an alias will not affect the original file. To rename a file, see page 52. To delete a file, see page 55.

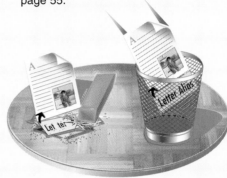

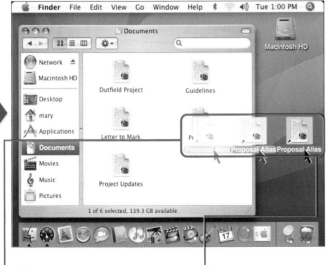

5 To move the alias to the desktop or to another location on your computer, position the mouse ▶ over the alias.

6 Drag the alias to the desktop or to another location.

■ The alias appears in the new location.

■ You can double-click the alias to open the original file at any time.

DUPLICATE A FILE

You can quickly create a duplicate of a file.

Creating a duplicate of a file is useful if you plan to make major changes to a file, but you want to keep a copy of the original file. Creating a duplicate gives you two copies of a file—the original file and a file that you can change.

You can duplicate a folder the same way you duplicate a file. When you duplicate a folder, all the files in the folder are also duplicated.

DUPLICATE A FILE

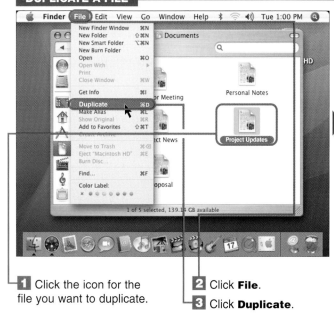

1 Click the icon for the file you want to duplicate.

2 Click **File**.

3 Click **Duplicate**.

■ A duplicate of the file appears. The word "copy" appears in the name of the duplicate file.

Note: To move the duplicate file to another location on your computer, see page 58. To rename the duplicate file, see page 52.

SEARCH FOR FILES USING SPOTLIGHT

If you cannot remember the exact name or location of a file you want to work with, you can use the new Spotlight feature to search for the file.

Mac OS X's new Spotlight feature allows you to instantly search your entire computer for files, as well as e-mail messages, address book contacts, images, applications and more.

SEARCH FOR FILES USING SPOTLIGHT

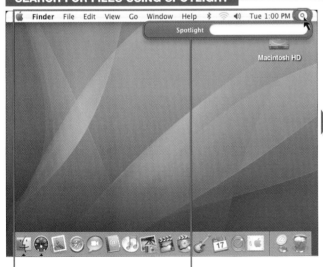

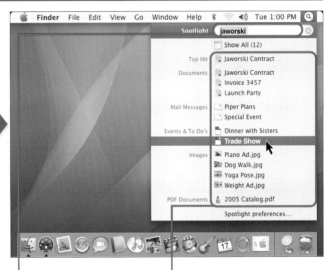

1 To search for a file on your computer, click .

■ The Spotlight area appears at the top of your screen.

2 Type information about the file you want to find, such as the file name or a word or phrase from within the file.

■ As you type, Spotlight displays a list of matching files and items on your computer.

3 To open a file, click the name of the file in the list.

PRINT A FILE

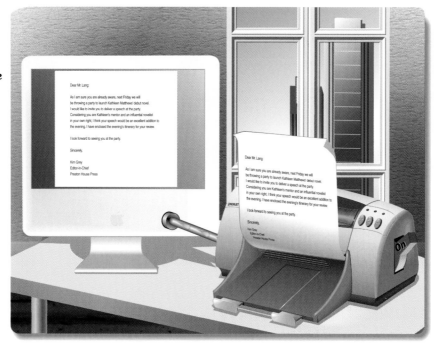

You can produce a paper copy of a file stored on your computer.

Before printing, make sure your printer is turned on and contains paper.

PRINT A FILE

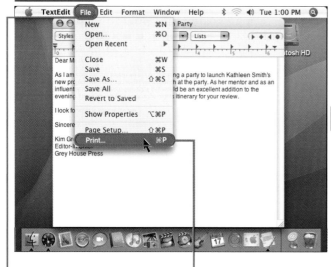

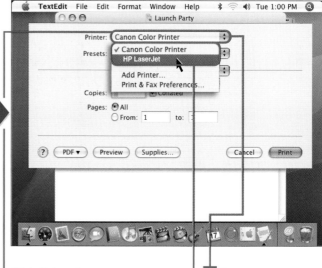

1 Open the file you want to print. To open a file, see page 50.

2 Click **File**.

3 Click **Print** to print the file.

Note: The name of the Print command depends on the active application.

■ A dialog sheet appears.

■ This area displays the printer your computer will use to print the file.

4 To change the printer your computer will use, click this area.

5 Click the printer you want to use to print the file.

Tip

Can I preview a file before printing?

Yes. You can preview a file to see how the file will look when printed. To preview a file, perform steps **1** to **3** below. In the dialog sheet that appears, click **Preview**. A window appears, displaying a preview of the file. If the file contains multiple pages, a miniature version of each page will appear on the side of the window. You can click the page you want to view. When you finish previewing the file, click ⬤ to close the window.

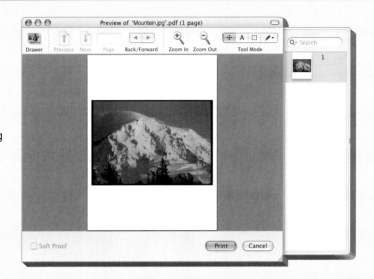

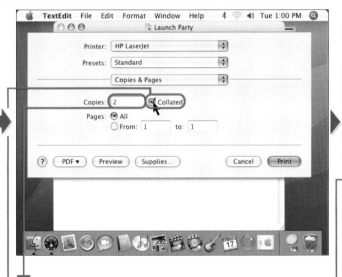

6 Double-click this area and type the number of copies of the file that you want to print.

7 If you chose to print more than one copy of the file, this option collates the copies. You can click this option to turn the option on (✅) or off (⬜).

Note: The Collated option prints the pages of each copy in order (1, 2, 1, 2). If you turn off the Collated option, the copies of each page will print together (1, 1, 2, 2).

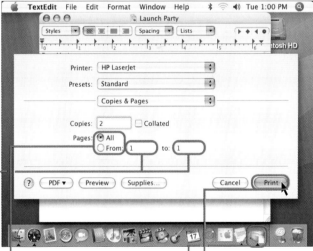

8 Click an option to specify if you want to print all the pages or a specific range of pages (◯ changes to ⬤).

■ If you selected From in step **8**, double-click this area and type the first page you want to print. Then press the `tab` key and type the last page you want to print.

9 Click **Print**.

■ A printer icon appears in the Dock. The printer icon disappears when the file has finished printing.

MANAGE FILES WAITING TO PRINT

You can view the status of files waiting to print. You can then pause the printing of a file, temporarily stop all files from printing or cancel the printing of a file.

VIEW FILES WAITING TO PRINT

1 Click the printer icon to view the status of the files waiting to print.

Note: If the printer icon is not displayed, the files have finished printing.

■ A window appears, displaying the status and name of each file waiting to print. The file at the top of the list will print first.

■ This area displays the status of the printer.

PAUSE A PRINT JOB

1 Click the name of the file you want to pause.

2 Click **Hold** to pause the print job.

3 When you are ready to resume printing a paused print job, click the name of the file you want to resume printing.

4 Click **Resume** to resume printing the file.

Tip

Why would I pause or stop a file from printing?

Pausing the printing of a file is useful when you want to allow more important files to print first.

Temporarily stopping all files from printing is useful when you want to change the toner or add more paper to the printer.

Stopping a file from printing is useful if you accidentally printed the wrong file or want to make last-minute changes to the file.

 Tip

Can I cancel the printing of several files at once?

Yes. To cancel the printing of several files at once, click the printer icon in the Dock to display the files waiting to print. Press and hold down the ⌘ key as you click the name of each file you no longer want to print. Then click **Delete** to cancel the print jobs.

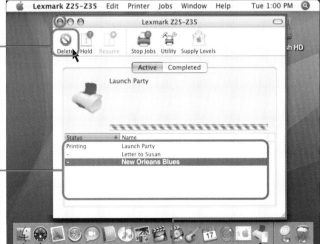

TEMPORARILY STOP ALL PRINT JOBS

1 To temporarily stop the printer from printing, click **Stop Jobs**.

Note: After you click Stop Jobs, the name of the button changes to Start Jobs and the status of the printer changes to "Jobs Stopped."

■ To resume printing, click **Start Jobs**.

CANCEL A PRINT JOB

1 Click the name of the file you no longer want to print.

2 Click **Delete** to cancel the print job.

■ The file disappears from the window and will no longer print.

CLOSE THE PRINTER WINDOW

1 When you finish managing the files waiting to print, click ⬤ to close the printer window.

VIEW PICTURES AND PDF FILES

You can use Preview to view pictures and Portable Document Format (PDF) files on your computer.

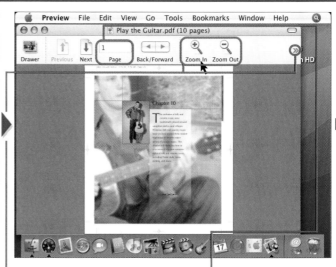

1 Double-click the picture or PDF file you want to view.

■ A window appears, displaying the picture or a page of the PDF file.

2 To magnify or reduce the size of the picture or page, click **Zoom In** or **Zoom Out**.

■ If the button you want to use is not displayed on the toolbar, click ≫ to display a list of the hidden buttons.

■ If you are viewing a PDF file that contains more than one page, this area displays the number of the current page.

What are PDF files?

A Portable Document Format (PDF) file is a popular file type that preserves a document's original layout and formatting. Books, product catalogs and support information for software are often distributed as PDF files, since this file type displays information exactly as it appears in printed form. PDF files are commonly found on the Web and on CDs included with books.

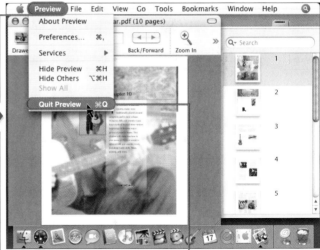

3 To display a miniature version of each page in the file, click **Drawer**.

■ A drawer opens, displaying each page in the file.

4 To view a different page, click the page you want to view.

■ You can also click **Previous** or **Next** to move backward or forward through the pages in the file.

Note: To close the drawer at any time, repeat step **3**.

5 When you finish viewing the picture or the contents of the PDF file, click **Preview**.

6 Click **Quit Preview**.

COPY FILES TO A CD OR DVD

You can copy files, such as pictures and movies, from your computer to a recordable CD or DVD.

You need a computer with a recordable CD or DVD drive to copy files to a CD or DVD.

If you want to copy only songs to a recordable CD, see page 164 for information on using iTunes to create a music CD.

COPY FILES TO A CD OR DVD

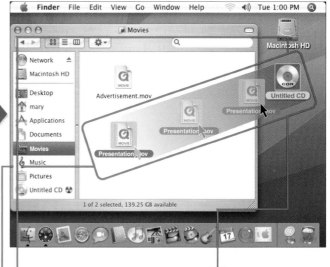

1 Insert a blank, recordable CD or DVD into your computer's recordable CD or DVD drive.

■ A dialog box appears, stating that you inserted a blank CD or DVD.

2 Click **OK** to continue.

■ An icon for the disc appears on the desktop.

3 Locate a file on your computer that you want to copy to the disc.

4 Position the mouse over the file you want to copy to the disc.

5 Drag the file to the disc's icon on the desktop.

6 Repeat steps **4** and **5** for each file you want to copy to the disc.

What types of discs can I copy files to?

If your computer has an Apple Combo drive, you can copy files to CD-R (CD-Recordable) and CD-RW (CD-ReWritable) discs. If your computer has an Apple SuperDrive, you can copy files to CD-R and CD-RW discs as well as DVD-R (DVD-Recordable) and DVD-RW (DVD-ReWritable) discs.

You can copy files to a CD-R or DVD-R disc only once and you cannot erase or change the contents of the disc. CD-RW and DVD-RW discs, however, allow you to erase the contents of the disc and copy new files to the disc.

Why would I copy files to a recordable CD or DVD?

You can copy files to a recordable CD or DVD to transfer large amounts of information between computers. You can also copy important files stored on your computer to a CD or DVD in case you accidentally erase the files or your computer fails.

7 To display the files you selected to copy to the disc, double-click the disc's icon.

■ A window appears, displaying the files you selected to copy to the disc.

Note: If the window displays a file you no longer want to copy to the disc, drag the file to the Trash icon in the Dock.

8 To copy the files to the disc, click **Burn**.

■ A dialog box appears, confirming that you want to burn the disc.

9 To create a name for the disc, drag the mouse $\mathcal{I}$ over the text in this area to select the text and then type a name.

10 Click **Burn** to copy the files to the disc.

■ A Burn dialog box appears, displaying the progress of the copy.

11 When the copy is complete, you can drag the disc's icon to the Trash icon in the Dock to eject the disc.

ERASE A CD-RW DISC

If a CD-RW (CD-ReWritable) disc contains information, you may need to erase the disc before you can copy new information to the disc.

Before erasing a CD-RW disc, make sure the disc does not contain information you want to keep. Erasing a CD-RW disc will permanently remove all the information from the disc.

ERASE A CD-RW DISC

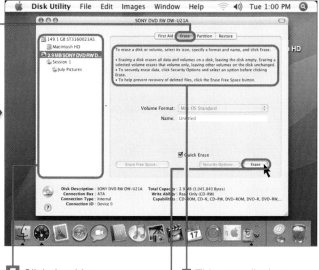

1 Insert the disc you want to erase into your computer's CD drive.

2 Click **Go**.

Note: If Go is not displayed, click a blank area on your desktop to display the Finder menu bar.

3 Click **Utilities** to view the utilities available on your computer.

■ The Utilities window appears.

4 Double-click **Disk Utility** to start Disk Utility.

5 Click the drive containing the disc you want to erase.

6 Click **Erase**.

■ This area displays information about erasing a disk.

7 Click **Erase** to erase the contents of the disc in the drive you selected.

Tip

Is there a limit to the number of times I can re-use a CD-RW disc?

Some CD-RW discs may no longer be able to store information after being erased many times. You should check the information that came with your disc to find out how many times you can safely erase and re-use the disc.

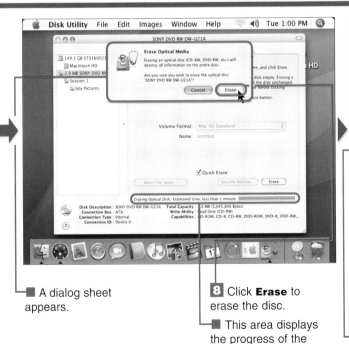

Tip

Can I erase a DVD-RW disc?

Yes. If your computer has a DVD-RW drive, you can perform the steps below to erase a DVD-RW disc to prepare the disc for storing new information. Before erasing a DVD-RW disc, make sure the disc does not contain information you want to keep.

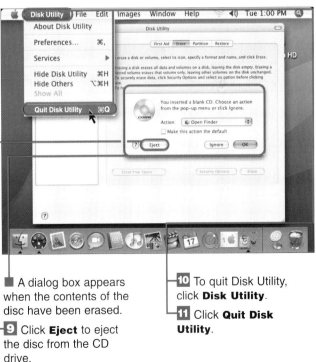

■ A dialog sheet appears.

8 Click **Erase** to erase the disc.

■ This area displays the progress of the erasing.

■ A dialog box appears when the contents of the disc have been erased.

9 Click **Eject** to eject the disc from the CD drive.

10 To quit Disk Utility, click **Disk Utility**.

11 Click **Quit Disk Utility**.

Slow   Fast

CHAPTER 4

Customize Your Computer

In this chapter, you will learn how to customize your computer by changing the screen saver, desktop picture and mouse settings. You will also learn how to turn on speech recognition so you can use spoken commands to perform tasks on your computer.

ADD OR REMOVE ICONS FROM THE DOCK

You can customize the Dock to include icons for the applications, folders and files you use most often. Adding icons to the Dock gives you quick access to these items at any time.

You can also remove icons for applications, folders and files that you do not frequently use. This helps reduce clutter in the Dock.

ADD AN ICON TO THE DOCK

1 Locate the application, folder or file you want to add to the Dock.

2 Position the mouse ▶ over the icon for the application, folder or file.

3 Drag the icon to the Dock.

Note: Drag applications to the left of the line in the Dock. Drag folders and files to the right of the line in the Dock.

■ The icon for the application, folder or file appears in the Dock.

Note: Adding an icon to the Dock does not remove the application, folder or file from its original location on your computer.

■ To open an application, folder or file displayed in the Dock, click its icon in the Dock.

Where can I find applications that I can add to the Dock?

You can find most of the applications available on your computer in the Applications folder.

Note: If Go is not available, click a blank area on your desktop to display the Finder menu bar.

2 Click **Applications**.

1 To display the contents of the Applications folder, click **Go**.

 How do I move an icon to a different location in the Dock?

To move an icon in the Dock, position the mouse ► over the icon and then drag the icon to a new location. The other icons in the Dock will move to make room for the icon. You cannot move the Finder or Trash icon. You also cannot move icons across the line in the Dock.

REMOVE AN ICON FROM THE DOCK

1 Position the mouse ► over the icon you want to remove from the Dock.

2 Drag the icon out of the Dock.

Note: You cannot remove the Finder ( ) or Trash ( ) icon from the Dock.

■ The icon disappears from the Dock in a puff of smoke.

■ When you remove the icon for an open application, the icon will not disappear from the Dock until you quit the application.

Note: Removing an icon from the Dock does not remove the application, folder or file from your computer.

CUSTOMIZE THE DOCK

You can change
the appearance
of the Dock and
the way the Dock
functions.

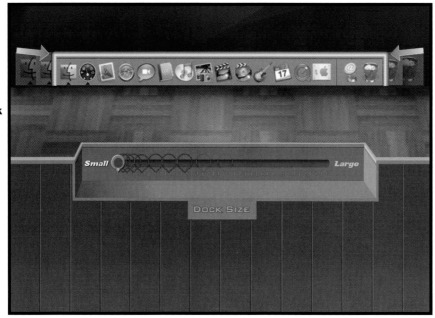

For example, you
can change the size
of the Dock and
stop application
icons in the Dock
from bouncing when
you click the icons.

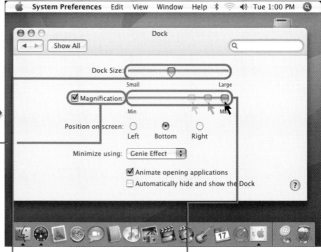

1 Click the System
Preferences icon to
access your system
preferences.

■ The System
Preferences window
appears.

2 Click **Dock** to
customize the Dock.

■ The Dock window
appears.

3 To decrease or increase
the size of the Dock, drag
this slider ( ) left or right.

4 This option magnifies
icons in the Dock when
you position the mouse ▶
over the icons. You can
click the option to turn the
option on (✓) or off ( ).

5 To decrease or increase
the amount of magnification
that will be used when you
position the mouse ▶ over
icons in the Dock, drag this
slider ( ) left or right.

Tip

Why would I use the Magnification option when customizing the Dock?

If you decrease the size of the Dock, you can use the Magnification option to magnify icons in the Dock when you position the mouse ▸ over the icons. This will allow you to clearly view an icon you are about to select in the Dock.

Tip

When the Dock is hidden, how do I redisplay the Dock?

To redisplay the Dock, position the mouse ▸ over the edge of your screen where the Dock last appeared. When you move the mouse ▸ away from the Dock, the Dock will disappear again.

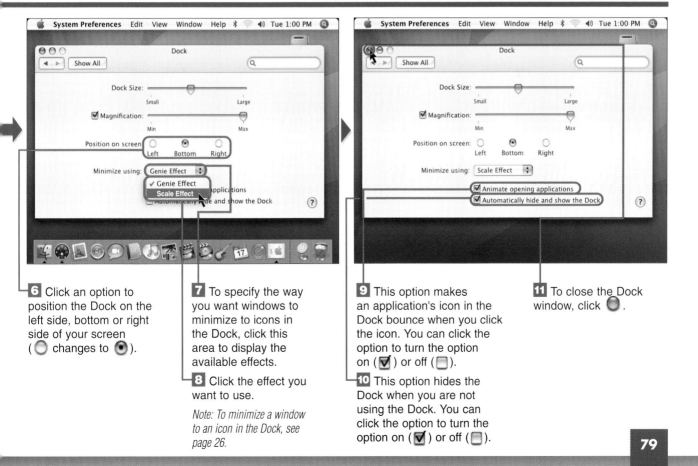

6 Click an option to position the Dock on the left side, bottom or right side of your screen (○ changes to ●).

7 To specify the way you want windows to minimize to icons in the Dock, click this area to display the available effects.

8 Click the effect you want to use.

Note: To minimize a window to an icon in the Dock, see page 26.

9 This option makes an application's icon in the Dock bounce when you click the icon. You can click the option to turn the option on (☑) or off (☐).

10 This option hides the Dock when you are not using the Dock. You can click the option to turn the option on (☑) or off (☐).

11 To close the Dock window, click ● .

CHANGE THE SCREEN SAVER

A screen saver is a picture or pattern that appears on the screen when you do not use your computer for a period of time.

You can use a screen saver to hide your work while you are away from your desk.

By default, a screen saver will appear on your screen when you do not use your computer for 20 minutes.

CHANGE THE SCREEN SAVER

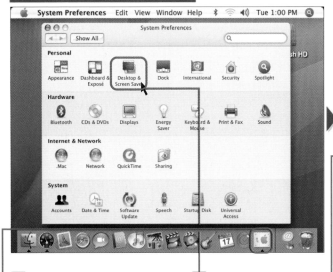

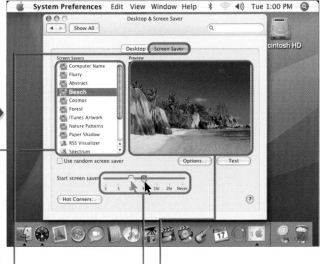

1 Click the System Preferences icon to access your system preferences.

■ The System Preferences window appears.

2 Click **Desktop & Screen Saver** to change your screen saver.

■ The Desktop & Screen Saver window appears.

3 Click **Screen Saver**.

4 Click the screen saver you want to use.

■ This area displays a preview of the screen saver.

5 To specify the number of minutes your computer must be inactive before the screen saver will start, drag this slider ( ) to the desired number of minutes.

*Note: If you never want the screen saver to start, drag the slider to **Never**.*

Tip

What are the .Mac and Pictures Folder screen savers?

The .Mac screen saver allows you to display a slide show published on the Internet by a .Mac member. After selecting the .Mac screen saver, you can click **Options** to specify the .Mac membership name of the person who published the slide show you want to use.

The Pictures Folder screen saver displays a slide show of the pictures in your Pictures folder. You can click **Choose Folder** to specify a different folder containing pictures you want to use.

Tip

Can I use a random screen saver?

Yes. You can have your computer automatically pick a screen saver for you each time the screen saver appears. Perform steps **1** to **3** below and then click **Use random screen saver** (changes to). Then perform step **10**.

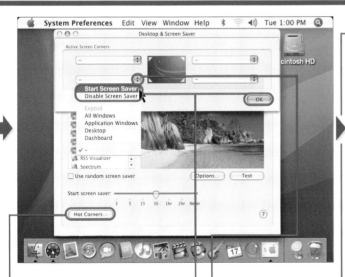

6 To create a hot corner on your screen that will start or turn off the screen saver when you position the mouse ➤ over the corner, click **Hot Corners**.

■ A dialog sheet appears.

7 Click ↕ beside the corner you want to make a hot corner.

8 Click an option to specify if you want the hot corner to start or disable the screen saver.

9 Click **OK** to save your changes.

10 To close the Desktop & Screen Saver window, click ●.

■ The screen saver appears when you do not use your computer for the number of minutes you specified.

■ You can move the mouse or press a key on the keyboard to remove the screen saver from your screen.

CHANGE THE DESKTOP PICTURE

You can change the picture used to decorate your desktop.

Mac OS X comes with several collections of pictures that you can choose from, including background images, nature pictures, abstract pictures and solid colors.

You can also display your own pictures on the desktop by selecting a picture from your Pictures folder.

CHANGE THE DESKTOP PICTURE

1 Click the System Preferences icon to access your system preferences.

■ The System Preferences window appears.

2 Click **Desktop & Screen Saver** to set up a screen saver.

■ The Desktop & Screen Saver window appears.

3 Click **Desktop**.

■ This area displays the picture currently displayed on your desktop.

4 Click a collection of pictures of interest.

■ This area displays the pictures that are available in the collection you selected.

5 Click the picture you want to display on your desktop.

Tip

How can I display a picture from the Pictures Folder collection on my desktop?

Mac OS X offers four ways you can display a picture from the Pictures Folder collection on your desktop.

Fill screen

Enlarges the picture to cover your entire desktop. The top and bottom edges of the picture may be cut off.

Stretch to fill screen

Stretches the picture to cover your entire desktop.

Center

Displays the picture in the middle of your desktop.

Tile

Repeats the picture until it fills your entire desktop.

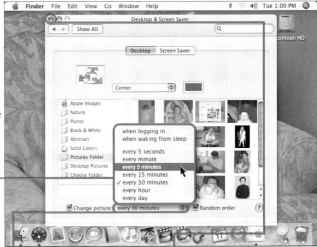

■ The picture you selected appears on your desktop.

6 If you selected a picture from the Pictures Folder collection, click this area to specify how you want to display the picture on your desktop.

7 Click the way you want to display the picture.

8 To have Mac OS X automatically change the desktop picture to other pictures in the same collection, click this option (🔲 changes to ☑).

9 To specify how often you want to change to a new picture, click this area.

10 Click the option you want to use.

11 To close the Desktop & Screen Saver window, click ⬤ .

■ To return to the original desktop picture, repeat steps **1** to **11**, selecting **Apple Images** in step **4** and **Aqua Blue** in step **5**.

CHANGE THE SCREEN RESOLUTION

You can change the screen resolution to adjust the amount of information that can fit on your screen.

Your monitor and video adapter determine which screen resolutions are available on your computer.

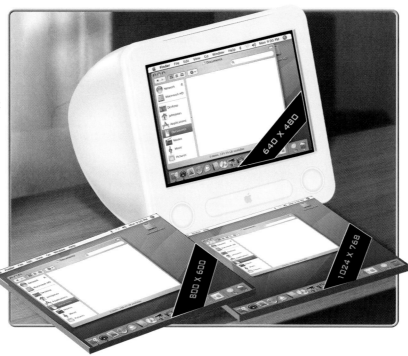

You will not usually change the resolution of a Liquid Crystal Display (LCD) monitor, since this can reduce the image quality. An LCD monitor is a thin, lightweight monitor compared to the bulkier Cathode Ray Tube (CRT) monitor.

CHANGE THE SCREEN RESOLUTION

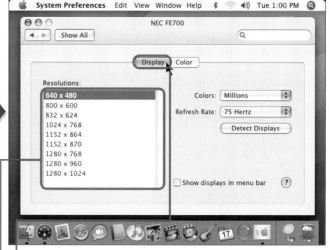

1 Click the System Preferences icon to access your system preferences.

■ The System Preferences window appears.

2 Click **Displays** to change your display settings.

■ The Display window appears, allowing you to change your display settings.

3 Click **Display**.

■ This area displays the resolutions available for your computer. The current resolution is highlighted.

Note: Each resolution may offer several refresh rates. The refresh rate is measured in hertz (Hz) and determines how often the screen is redrawn. A higher refresh rate reduces screen flicker and eyestrain.

Tip

Which screen resolution should I use?

The screen resolution is measured by the number of horizontal and vertical pixels displayed on a screen. A pixel is the smallest point on a screen. The screen resolution you should choose depends on the size of your monitor and the amount of information you want to view on your screen at once.

Lower screen resolutions display larger images so you can see the information on your screen more clearly.

Higher resolutions display smaller images so you can display more information on your screen at once.

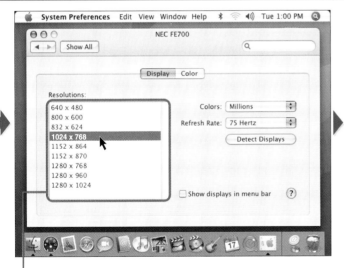

4 Click the resolution you want to use.

*Note: If you choose a lower resolution than the resolution that is currently displayed, a dialog box may appear. Click **OK** to change the resolution.*

■ Mac OS X resizes the information on your screen.

■ A confirmation dialog box may appear, asking if you want to keep the new screen resolution. Click **Confirm** or **Revert** to specify if you want to use the new resolution.

5 To close the Display window, click ⬤ .

CHANGE THE DATE OR TIME

You should make sure the correct date and time are set in your computer. Mac OS X uses the date and time to determine when you create and update your files.

Your computer has a built-in clock that keeps track of the date and time even when you turn off the computer.

CHANGE THE DATE OR TIME

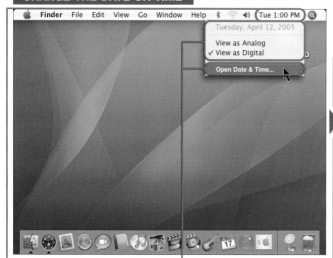

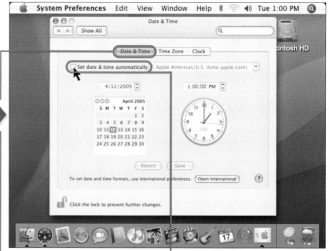

■ This area displays the day and time set in your computer.

1 To display the date set in your computer, click this area.

■ A menu appears, displaying the current date.

2 To change the date or time set in your computer, click **Open Date & Time**.

■ The Date & Time window appears.

3 Click **Date & Time** to change the date or time.

■ This option automatically synchronizes your computer's clock with a time server on the Internet. To change the date or time yourself, click this option to turn the option off (☑ changes to ☐).

Will Mac OS X ever change the time automatically?

Mac OS X will change the time automatically to compensate for daylight saving time. When you turn on your computer after daylight saving time occurs, Mac OS X will have automatically changed the time.

How can I change the time zone set in my computer?

Perform steps 1 to 3 on page 86, except select **Time Zone** in step 3. Drag the mouse over the text in the Closest City area and then type the first few letters of the name of a major city close to you in your time zone. Mac OS X automatically completes the city name for you. Continue typing until the city name you want appears in the area and then press the return key. A grey area on the map indicates the time zone you selected.

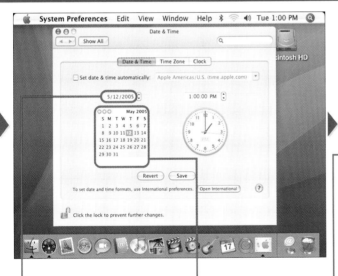

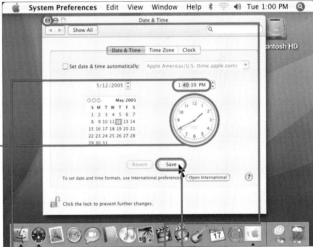

4 This area displays the current date. To change the date, click the part of the date you want to change and then type the correct information.

■ This area displays the days in the current month. The current day is highlighted.

5 This area displays the current time. To change the time, click the part of the time you want to change and type the correct information.

■ The clock in this area displays the current time.

6 To save the changes you made to the date and time, click **Save**.

7 To close the Date & Time window, click ◯.

CHANGE THE LOOK OF THE CLOCK

Mac OS X allows you to specify how you want to display the time on your computer.

By default, the time is displayed in the menu bar in digital format. You can choose to display the time in a floating window or in analog format instead.

CHANGE THE LOOK OF THE CLOCK

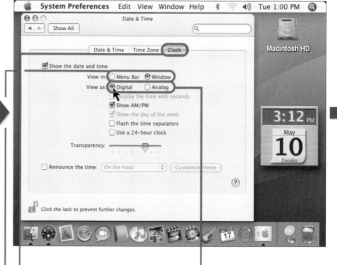

1 Click the System Preferences icon to access your system preferences.

■ The System Preferences window appears.

2 Click **Date & Time** to change the look of the clock.

■ The Date & Time window appears.

3 Click **Clock**.

4 Click an option to specify if you want to show the time in the menu bar or in a floating window on your desktop (◯ changes to ◉).

5 Click an option to specify if you want to display the time in a digital or analog format (◯ changes to ◉).

Tip

Can I move the clock that floats on my desktop?

To move the clock to a new location on your desktop, position the mouse ▶ over the floating clock and then drag the clock to a new location.

Tip

I no longer want to display a floating clock on my desktop. How do I remove the clock?

To remove the floating clock from your desktop, perform steps **1** to **4** below, selecting **Menu Bar** in step **4**. Then perform step **11**.

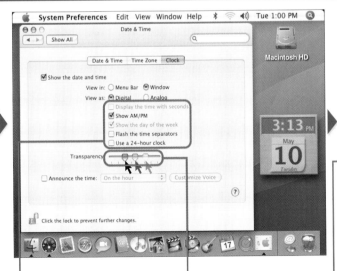

6 These options affect the appearance of the date and time. You can click an option to turn the option on (☑) or off (☐).

*Note: The available options depend on the options you selected in steps **4** and **5**.*

7 If you selected to show the time in a floating window on your desktop, you can drag this slider (◯) to change the transparency of the window.

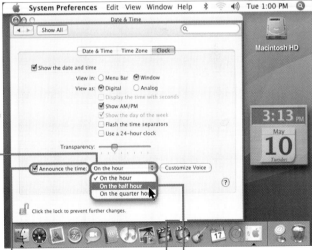

8 To have your computer say the time at specified intervals, click this option (☐ changes to ☑).

9 To specify how often your computer will say the time, click this area.

10 Click an option to specify how often your computer will say the time.

11 To close the Date & Time window, click ◯ .

ADD A PRINTER

Before you can use a printer, you need to add the printer to your computer. You need to add a printer only once.

ADD A PRINTER

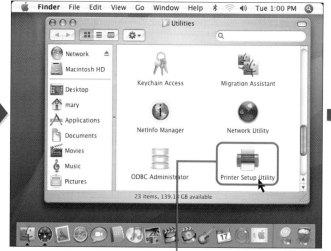

1 Click **Go**.

Note: If Go is not available, click a blank area on your desktop to display the Finder menu bar.

2 Click **Utilities** to view the utility applications available on your computer.

■ The Utilities window appears, displaying the utility applications available on your computer.

3 Double-click **Printer Setup Utility** to manage your printers.

Note: You can click ● in the Utilities window to close the window.

Tip

I am having trouble adding a printer. What should I do?

If you are having trouble adding a printer, Mac OS X may not have the software required to communicate with the printer. To add the printer, install the software included with the printer. If your printer did not come with software, you may be able to download the correct software from the printer manufacturer's Web site.

 Tip

How do I change the default printer?

The default printer automatically prints all your files. To change the default printer, perform steps **1** to **3** on page 90 to display the Printer List window. Click the name of the printer you want to make the default printer and then click **Make Default**. The name of the default printer appears in **bold** type.

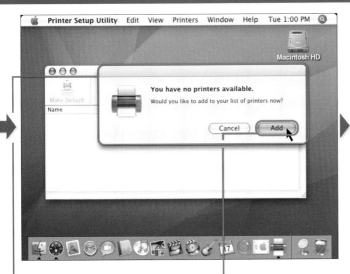

■ The Printer List window appears.

■ If you do not have any printers installed on your computer, a dialog box appears, stating that you have no printers available on your computer.

4 Click **Add** to add a printer.

*Note: If the dialog box does not appear, click **Add** in the Printer List window to add a printer.*

■ The Printer Browser window appears.

■ This area displays the printers currently connected to your computer and the type of connection the printer uses.

CONTINUED

ADD A PRINTER

When you add a
printer, your computer
can locate the printers
available to you and
then display the
printers in a list for
you to choose from.

ADD A PRINTER (CONTINUED)

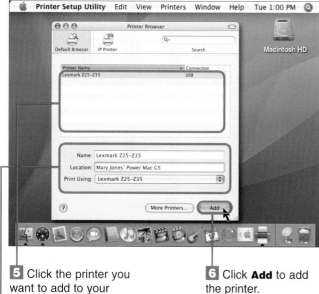

5 Click the printer you
want to add to your
computer.

■ This area displays
information about the
printer, such as the printer's
name and location.

6 Click **Add** to add
the printer.

■ The printer appears
in the Printer List
window.

■ You can now use
the printer to print
documents on your
computer.

7 To quit Printer
Setup Utility, click
Printer Setup Utility.

8 Click **Quit Printer
Setup Utility**.

CHANGE THE KEYBOARD SETTINGS

You can change the way your keyboard responds to the keys you type.

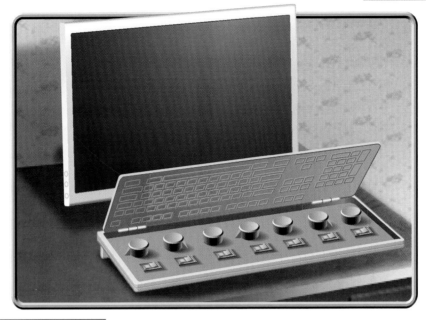

For example, you can change how fast a character repeats when you hold down a key on your keyboard.

CHANGE THE KEYBOARD SETTINGS

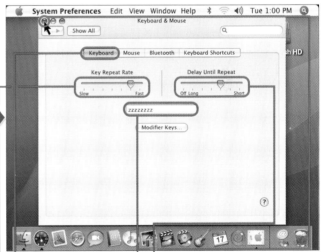

1 Click the **System Preferences** icon to access your system preferences.

■ The System Preferences window appears.

2 Click **Keyboard & Mouse** to change your keyboard settings.

■ The Keyboard & Mouse window appears.

3 Click **Keyboard**.

4 To change how quickly characters repeat when you hold down a key, drag this slider (⬤) to a new position.

5 To change how long you must hold down a key before the character starts repeating, drag this slider (⬤) to a new position.

6 To test the keyboard settings, drag the mouse ⊺ over the text in this area and then press and hold down a key on your keyboard.

7 To close the Keyboard & Mouse window, click ⬤.

93

CHANGE THE MOUSE SETTINGS

You can change the way your mouse works to make the mouse easier to use.

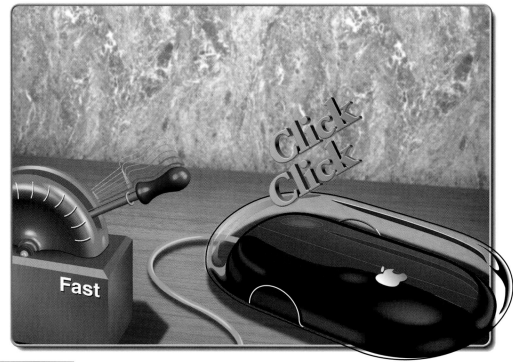

You can change how fast the mouse pointer moves on your screen and the speed at which you can double-click an item to open the item.

CHANGE THE MOUSE SETTINGS

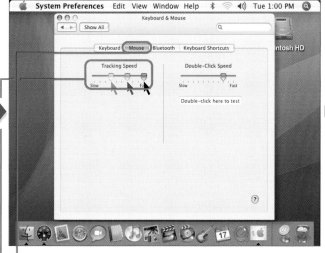

1 Click the System Preferences icon to access your system preferences.

■ The System Preferences window appears.

2 Click **Keyboard & Mouse** to change your mouse settings.

■ The **Keyboard & Mouse** window appears.

3 Click **Mouse**.

4 To change how fast the mouse ⬆ moves on your screen, drag this slider (🔵) to a new position.

Note: If you perform detailed work, you may want to use a slower speed. If you have a large monitor, you may want to use a faster speed.

Tip

Should I use a mouse pad?

When you use a mechanical mouse, which detects movement using a ball on the bottom of the mouse, a mouse pad provides a smooth, flat surface for moving the mouse and helps reduce the amount of dirt that enters the mouse. When you use an optical mouse, which detects movement using a beam of light, you do not need to use a mouse pad. For the best results when using an optical mouse, you should use the mouse on a flat surface that is a solid color.

Mechanical Mouse   **Optical Mouse**

Tip

Can I make my optical mouse easier to click?

If a ring surrounds the light on the bottom of your optical mouse, you can turn the ring to adjust the click tension and make the mouse easier to click. The - setting reduces the click tension, making the mouse easier to click. The **o** setting provides moderate click tension and the **+** setting provides the highest click tension.

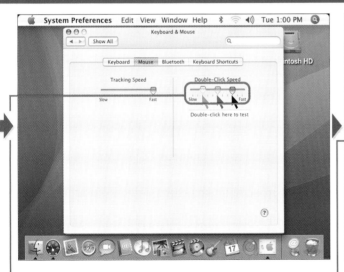

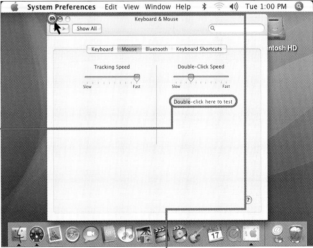

5 To change the amount of time that can pass between two clicks of the mouse button for Mac OS X to recognize a double-click, drag this slider (⬙) to a new position.

Note: If you have difficulty using the mouse, you may want to use a slower double-click speed.

6 To test the new double-click speed, double-click the text in this area.

■ Text in this area is highlighted when you double-click at the correct speed.

7 To close the Keyboard & Mouse window, click ⬤.

CHANGE THE ENERGY SAVING SETTINGS

You can change the energy saving settings for your computer. These settings allow you to specify how long your computer must be inactive before automatically going to sleep to conserve power.

By default, your computer automatically goes to sleep when you do not use the computer for 10 minutes. When your computer goes to sleep, your screen will turn black.

CHANGE THE ENERGY SAVING SETTINGS

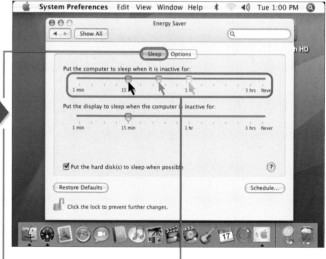

1 Click the System Preferences icon to access your system preferences.

■ The System Preferences window appears.

2 Click **Energy Saver** to change your energy saving settings.

■ The Energy Saver window appears.

3 Click **Sleep**.

4 To change the amount of time your computer must be inactive before automatically going to sleep, drag this slider ( ) to a new position.

*Note: If you never want the computer to automatically go to sleep, drag the slider to **Never**.*

How can I wake a sleeping computer?

To wake a sleeping computer, move the mouse or press a key on your keyboard. When you wake the computer, any open applications and files will appear as you left them. You may have to wait several seconds for the computer to wake.

Why did this warning message appear in the Energy Saver window?

This warning message appears when you specify an amount of time in step **4** or **5** that is shorter than the amount of time your computer must be inactive before the screen saver starts. You may want to change when the screen saver starts so the screen saver will appear before your computer goes to sleep. For information on changing a screen saver, see page 80.

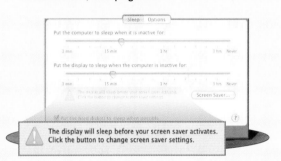

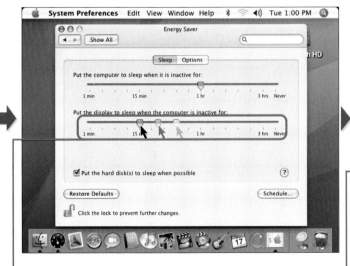

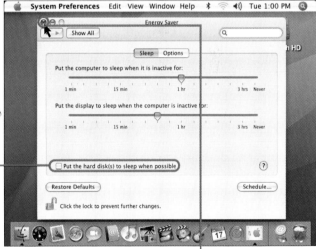

5 To change the amount of time your computer must be inactive before the display goes to sleep, drag this slider (⬭) to a new position.

Note: You cannot specify a longer amount of time for the display than you specified for the computer in step 4.

6 This option puts your hard disk to sleep whenever possible. You can click the option to turn the option on (☑) or off (☐).

7 To close the Energy Saver window, click ⬤.

OPEN AN APPLICATION AUTOMATICALLY

If you use the same application every day, you can have the application open automatically each time you log in to Mac OS X.

You can also set up files and folders to open automatically each time you log in the same way you set up applications.

OPEN AN APPLICATION AUTOMATICALLY

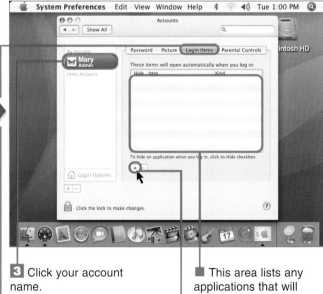

1 Click the System Preferences icon to access your system preferences.

■ The System Preferences window appears.

2 Click **Accounts** to access information for your user account.

■ The Accounts window appears.

3 Click your account name.

4 Click **Login Items** to specify the applications you want to open automatically when you log in.

■ This area lists any applications that will open automatically when you log in.

5 To add an application to the list, click +.

■ A dialog sheet appears.

How do I stop an application from opening automatically?

To stop an application from opening automatically, you must remove the application from the Accounts window. Removing an application from the Accounts window will not remove the application from your computer.

1 Perform steps **1** to **4** below to display the list of applications that open automatically.

2 Click the application you no longer want to open automatically when you log in.

3 Click $-$ to remove the application from the window.

4 To close the Accounts window, click ⬤ .

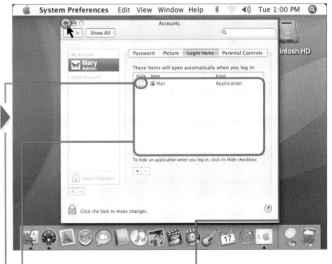

■ This area shows the location of the displayed applications. You can click this area to change the location.

6 Click the application you want to open automatically when you log in.

■ This area displays information about the application you selected.

7 Click **Add** to add the application to the list.

■ The application appears in this area.

■ To have Mac OS X automatically hide an application after the application is opened, click the check box beside the application's name (☐ changes to ☑).

8 To close the Accounts window, click ⬤ .

CHANGE THE SOUND SETTINGS

You can change your computer's sound settings to suit your preferences. For example, you can change the alert sound your computer uses and adjust the volume of sound on the computer.

Your computer uses the alert sound to get your attention or notify you of a problem.

CHANGE THE SOUND SETTINGS

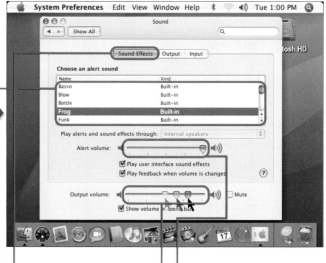

1 Click the System Preferences icon to access your system preferences.

■ The System Preferences window appears.

2 Click **Sound** to change your computer's sound settings.

■ The Sound window appears.

3 Click **Sound Effects**.

4 Click the sound you want to use for alerts. The alert sound you selected plays.

5 To decrease or increase the alert volume, drag this slider ( ) left or right. The new alert sound plays at the new volume.

6 To decrease or increase the computer's volume, drag this slider ( ) left or right. The current alert sound plays at the new volume.

How do I change my computer's volume using the speaker icon (◀))) in the menu bar?

To change your computer's volume, click the speaker icon (◀))) in the menu bar. On the volume control bar that appears, drag the slider (●) up or down to increase or decrease your computer's volume.

How can I turn off the sound on my computer?

To turn off the sound on your computer, perform steps **1** to **3** below to display the Sound window. Click **Mute** to turn off the sound on your computer (◻ changes to ☑). To once again turn on the sound, click **Mute** again (☑ changes to ◻).

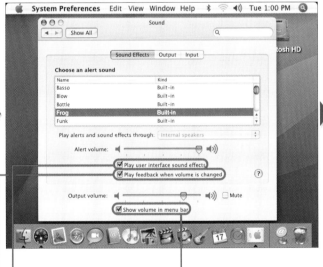

■ This option plays a sound when you perform certain actions on your computer, such as deleting a file.

■ This option plays a sound when you press a volume key on your keyboard.

■ This option allows you to adjust the volume of your computer using a speaker icon (◀))) in the menu bar.

7 You can click an option to turn the option on (☑) or off (◻).

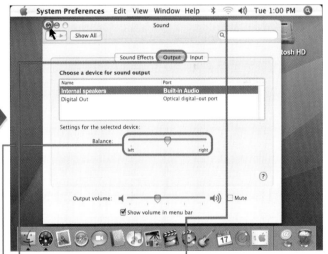

8 Click the **Output** tab.

9 To adjust the balance between your left and right speakers, drag this slider (▽) left or right.

Note: Changing the balance between your speakers increases the volume of one speaker while decreasing the volume of the other speaker.

10 To close the Sound window, click ● .

USING SPEECH RECOGNITION

You can turn on speech recognition to use spoken commands to control your computer.

Using spoken commands can help save you time when performing tasks on your computer since one spoken command often performs several steps.

TURN ON SPEECH RECOGNITION

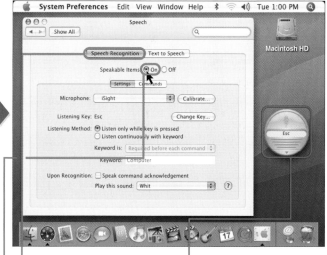

1 Click the System Preferences icon to access your system preferences.

■ The System Preferences window appears.

2 Click **Speech** to turn on speech recognition.

■ The Speech window appears.

3 Click **Speech Recognition**.

4 To turn on speech recognition, click **On** (○ changes to ●).

*Note: The first time you turn on speech recognition, a dialog sheet appears, displaying tips on using speech recognition. You can click **Continue** to close the dialog sheet.*

■ When speech recognition is turned on, the Speech Feedback window appears on your screen.

Tip

How can I make speech recognition completely hands-free?

If you do not want to press the `esc` key each time you give your computer a spoken command, you can have the computer respond to a spoken keyword instead. Perform steps **1** to **4** below and then click **Listen continuously with keyword** (⭘ changes to ⊙). You can then say the keyword "Computer" before each spoken

command you give to the computer instead of pressing the `esc` key. For more information on giving your computer spoken commands, see page 104.

Tip

How do I turn off speech recognition?

If you no longer want to use spoken commands to control your computer, you can turn off speech recognition at any time. Perform steps **1** to **4** below, selecting **Off** in step **4**. Then perform step **8**.

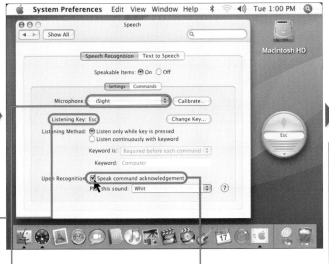

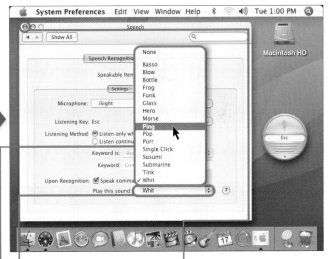

■ This area displays the microphone you will speak into when giving commands to your computer. You can click this area to select a different microphone.

■ This area displays the name of the keyboard key you must press when giving your computer a spoken command. By default, the key you must press is the `esc` key.

5 To have your computer repeat your spoken commands, click this option (☐ changes to ☑).

6 To specify the sound you want to play each time your computer recognizes a spoken command, click this area to display a list of the available sounds.

7 Click the sound you want to play. The sound you selected plays.

8 To close the Speech window, click ⭘.

■ You can now use spoken commands to control your computer. To use spoken commands, see page 104.

CONTINUED

USING SPEECH RECOGNITION

When speech recognition is turned on, you can use spoken commands to perform tasks on your computer, such as closing a window, opening an application or starting your screen saver.

You need to connect a microphone to your computer to use spoken commands to perform tasks on the computer.

USE SPOKEN COMMANDS

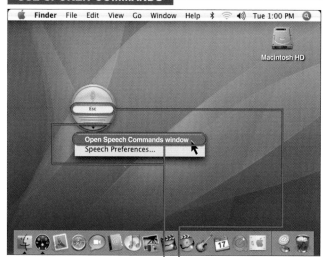

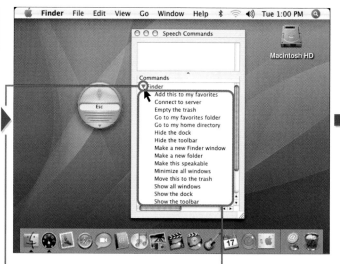

■ When speech recognition is turned on, the Speech Feedback window appears on your screen.

Note: To turn on speech recognition, see page 102.

■ This area displays the name of the key you can press and hold down to have your computer listen to your spoken commands.

1 To display a list of spoken commands you can use, click ▼.

2 Click **Open Speech Commands window**.

■ The Speech Commands window appears, displaying the categories of commands you can use.

Note: The available categories depend on the active application.

3 You can click ▶ beside a category to display the commands in the category (▶ changes to ▼).

■ The commands in the category appear.

■ You can click ▼ to once again hide the commands in the category.

How should I speak to my computer when using spoken commands?

You should speak to your computer in your normal tone of voice, pronouncing words clearly and not pausing between words. You should also speak at a consistent volume so the bars in the Speech Feedback window are primarily green. If you speak too softly or too loudly, the computer may not be able to recognize your commands.

Can I minimize the Speech Feedback window?

Yes. To minimize the Speech Feedback window to an icon in the Dock, double-click the window or press and hold down the esc key as you say "Minimize Speech Feedback window." To redisplay the window, click the icon for the window in the Dock.

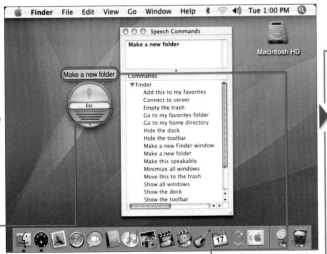

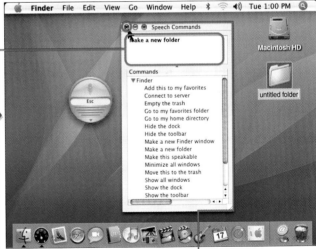

4 Press and hold down the esc key and then speak a command into your microphone.

■ While you speak, bars in the Speech Feedback window indicate the sound level of your voice.

Note: The bars should be green. If a red bar appears, you are speaking too loudly.

■ Your spoken command appears in a yellow box above the Speech Feedback window and a sound plays.

Note: Your computer may also repeat your spoken command.

■ This area of the Speech Commands window displays your spoken commands in bold.

■ You can repeat step **4** for each spoken command you want to use.

5 To close the Speech Commands window, click ⊙.

■ To turn off speech recognition, you can say "Quit speakable items."

CHANGE THE WAY YOUR COMPUTER SPEAKS

You can change the voice your computer uses to speak. Mac OS X offers several different voices you can choose from.

CHANGE THE WAY YOUR COMPUTER SPEAKS

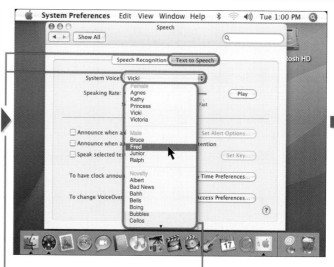

1 Click the System Preferences icon to access your system preferences.

■ The System Preferences window appears.

2 Click **Speech** to change the way your computer speaks.

■ The Speech window appears.

3 To change the voice your computer uses to speak, click **Text to Speech**.

4 This area displays the voice your computer uses to speak. Click this area to display other voices you can choose.

5 Click the voice you want your computer to use.

106

Tip

When will my computer use the voice I select?

Your computer will use the voice you select to read aloud text in applications such as TextEdit. To have your computer read aloud in a TextEdit document, see the top of page 141. Your computer will also use the voice to speak when you use features such as speech recognition. For information on using speech recognition, see page 102.

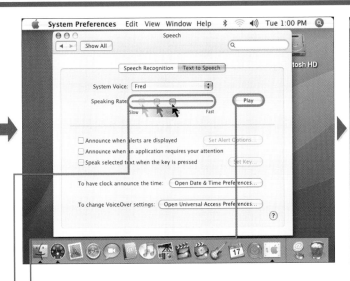

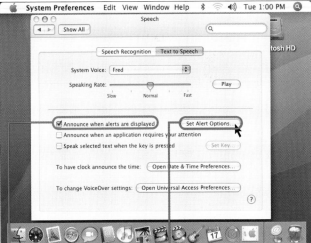

6 Click **Play** to hear your computer speak using the new voice.

7 To have the computer speak slower or faster, drag this slider ( ) left or right.

■ You can repeat step **6** to hear your computer speak using the new speed.

8 To have your computer announce when an alert is displayed on your screen, click this option (changes to ☑).

9 To change the way the computer makes the announcement, click **Set Alert Options**.

■ A dialog sheet appears.

CONTINUED

CHANGE THE WAY YOUR COMPUTER SPEAKS

You can have
your computer
read the text in
alerts that appear
on your screen.

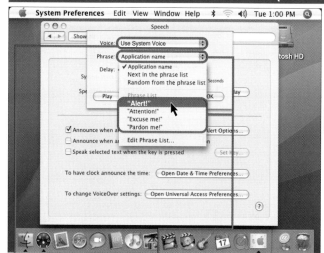

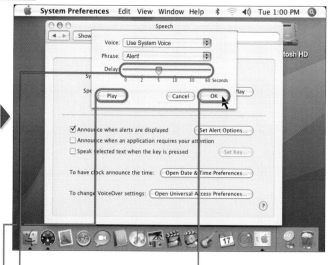

■ This area displays
the voice the computer
will use to announce an
alert. You can click this
area to select a different
voice.

10 This area displays the
phrase the computer will
speak when an alert
appears. Click this area to
display other phrases you
can choose.

11 Click the phrase you
want your computer to use.

12 To specify how long
your computer should
wait before speaking
when an alert appears,
drag this slider (⬤) to
a new position.

13 Click **Play** to hear
the way your computer
will announce an alert.

14 Click **OK** to
confirm the alert
options you selected.

Tip

Which phrase should I have my computer speak when an alert appears?

If you cannot decide which phrase you want your computer to speak in step **11** below, you can have your computer choose a phrase for you. Click **Next in the phrase list** to have your computer choose a phrase in order from the list each time an alert appears. Click **Random from the phrase list** to have your computer randomly choose a phrase from the list each time an alert appears.

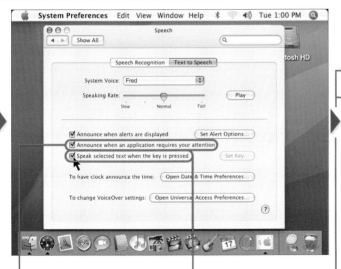

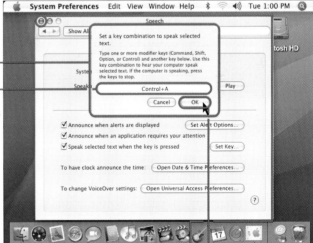

15 To have your computer announce when an application needs your attention, click this option (☐ changes to ☑).

16 To have your computer read aloud selected text in an application when you type a specific keyboard shortcut, click this option (☐ changes to ☑).

■ A dialog sheet appears, allowing you to specify the keyboard shortcut you want to use.

*Note: If the dialog sheet does not appear, click **Set Key** to display the dialog sheet.*

17 Type the keyboard shortcut, such as control + A, that you want to use to tell the computer to read selected text.

18 Click **OK** to confirm the keyboard shortcut you entered.

19 To close the Speech window, click ⬤.

CHANGE UNIVERSAL ACCESS SETTINGS

If you have vision, hearing or mobility impairments, Mac OS X offers many accessibility options that can help make your computer easier to use.

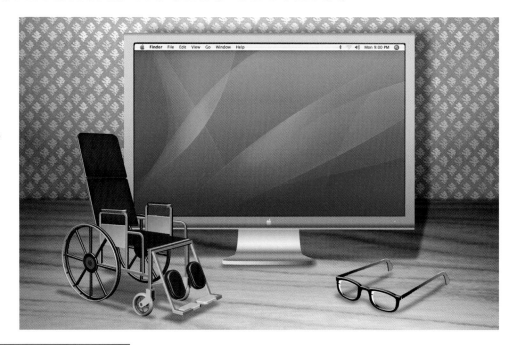

CHANGE UNIVERSAL ACCESS SETTINGS

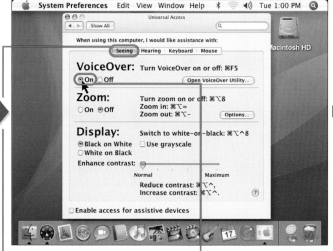

1 Click the System Preferences icon to access your system preferences.

■ The System Preferences window appears.

2 Click **Universal Access** to change your universal access settings.

■ The Universal Access window appears.

Note: Changes you make in the window will immediately affect your computer.

3 If you have difficulty seeing the information on your screen, click **Seeing**.

4 To turn on VoiceOver so you can hear a spoken description of items on your computer screen, click **On** (◯ changes to ◉).

Tip

What types of items on my screen will VoiceOver describe for me?

VoiceOver reads aloud the items on your screen, such as the contents of active windows, dialog boxes and open documents. VoiceOver is useful if you have difficulty reading the information displayed on your screen.

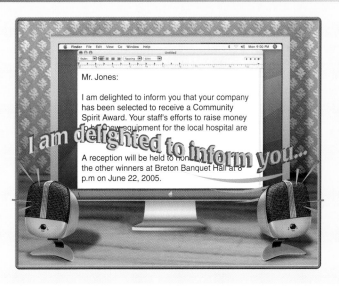

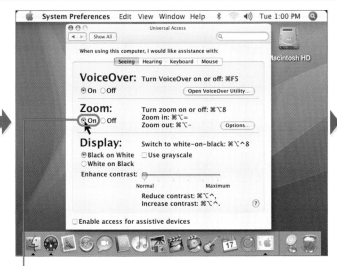

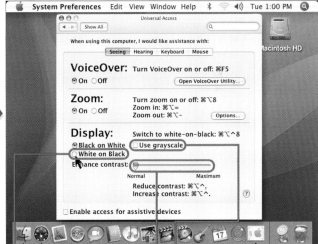

5 To turn on Zoom so you can magnify an area of your screen, click **On** (○ changes to ●).

■ To magnify an area of your screen, position the mouse ▶ over the area and then press and hold down the [option] and [⌘] keys as you press the = key. To reduce the magnification, press and hold down the [option] and [⌘] keys as you press the – key.

6 To display your screen with white text on a black background, click **White on Black** (○ changes to ●).

*Note: You can click **Black on White** to return to the original screen setting.*

7 To display your screen in shades of gray instead of colors, click **Use grayscale** (☐ changes to ☑).

8 To change the amount of contrast displayed on your screen, drag this slider (○) to the left or right.

CONTINUED

CHANGE UNIVERSAL ACCESS SETTINGS

Mac OS X offers accessibility settings that can help people who have difficulty hearing computer sounds and pressing keys on the keyboard.

CHANGE UNIVERSAL ACCESS SETTINGS (CONTINUED)

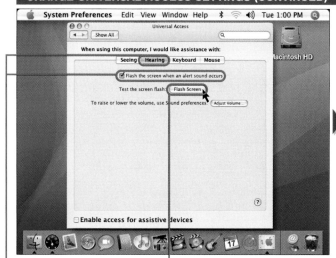

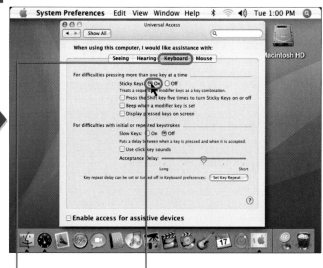

9 If you have difficulty hearing sounds on your computer, click **Hearing**.

10 To have your screen flash when an alert sounds, click this option (☐ changes to ☑).

Note: Your computer uses alert sounds to get your attention or notify you of a problem.

11 To preview how your screen will flash, click **Flash Screen**.

12 If you have difficulty using your keyboard, click **Keyboard**.

13 Sticky Keys allows you to press the shift , control , option or ⌘ key and have the key remain active while you press another key. To turn on Sticky Keys, click **On** (◯ changes to ⦿).

Note: Sticky Keys is useful for people who have difficulty pressing two keys at the same time.

Tip

When Sticky Keys is turned on, how will the symbols for keys I press appear on my screen?

When you press the shift , control , option or ⌘ key, the key's symbol appears and remains on your screen until you complete the keyboard shortcut, such as ⌘ + Q . If you no longer want to use the key, press the key twice to remove the key's symbol from your screen.

Key	Symbol
shift	⇧
control	⌃
option	⌥
⌘	⌘

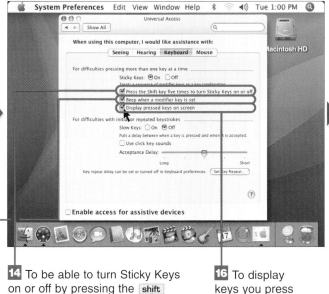

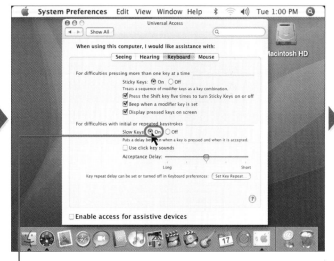

14 To be able to turn Sticky Keys on or off by pressing the shift key five times, click this option (☐ changes to ☑).

15 To have a sound play when you press the shift , control , option or ⌘ key, click this option (☐ changes to ☑).

16 To display keys you press on your screen, click this option (☐ changes to ☑).

17 Slow Keys allows you to add a delay between when you press a key and when the key is accepted. To turn on Slow Keys, click **On** (○ changes to ●).

Note: Slow Keys is useful for people who often press keys for too long.

CONTINUED

If you have trouble
using the mouse
to navigate your
computer, you can
select accessibility
options that allow
you to use the
keyboard to move
the mouse pointer
on your screen.

CHANGE UNIVERSAL ACCESS SETTINGS (CONTINUED)

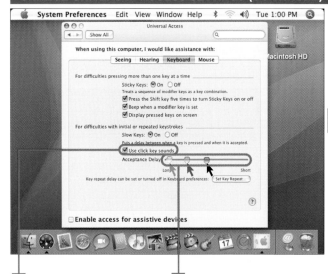

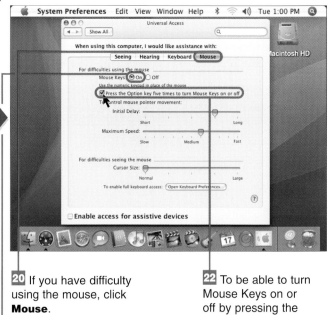

18 To have a sound
play when you press
a key, click this option
(☐ changes to ☑).

19 To change the amount of
time the computer must wait
before accepting a key you
press, drag this slider (⬤)
to the left or right.

20 If you have difficulty
using the mouse, click
Mouse.

21 Mouse Keys allows you
to use the numeric keypad
on the right side of your
keyboard to control the
mouse ⬉ on your screen.
To turn on Mouse Keys, click
On (◯ changes to ⬤).

22 To be able to turn
Mouse Keys on or
off by pressing the
option key five times,
click this option
(☐ changes to ☑).

Tip

After I turn on Mouse Keys, what keys on the numeric keypad can I use to control the mouse ▶?

Mouse Action	Key to Press
Move left or right	Press 4 or 6
Move down or up	Press 2 or 8
Move diagonally	Press 1 , 3 , 7 or 9
Click	Press 5
Double-click	Press 5 twice
Hold down the mouse button	Press 0
Release the mouse button	Press .

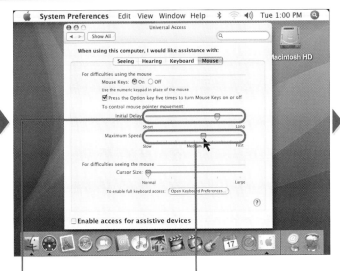

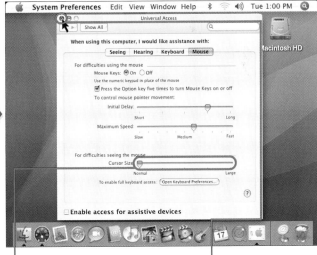

23 To change how quickly the mouse ▶ starts moving on your screen when you press a key, drag this slider (◉) to the left or right.

24 To change how quickly the mouse ▶ moves on your screen when you press a key, drag this slider (◉) to the left or right.

25 To change the size of the mouse ▶ displayed on your screen, drag this slider (◉) to the left or right.

26 To close the Universal Access window, click ◉.

ADD A BLUETOOTH DEVICE

What is Bluetooth?

Bluetooth wireless technology allows computers and devices to communicate without cables. Bluetooth devices use radio signals to transmit information and operate over a distance of up to 30 feet. Bluetooth was named after a tenth-century Danish king named Harald Bluetooth.

Can my computer use Bluetooth devices?

Computers do not usually come with the capability to use Bluetooth devices. To add Bluetooth capability to a computer, you can plug in an external Bluetooth adapter, or module, to a computer. Once you add Bluetooth capability to a computer, any Bluetooth device can communicate with the computer.

How can I use Bluetooth technology?

✓ Use a Bluetooth wireless mouse or keyboard to prevent clutter on your desk.

✓ Connect wirelessly to the Internet using a Bluetooth cell phone when traveling with a notebook computer.

✓ Print to a Bluetooth wireless printer.

✓ Use a Bluetooth wireless headset to control your computer using voice commands.

✓ Transfer information between a computer and a Personal Digital Assistant (PDA), such as a Palm handheld device.

What must I do before adding a Bluetooth device to my computer?

✓ If your computer does not have built-in Bluetooth capability, attach a Bluetooth adapter, or module, to your computer.

✓ Insert batteries into the Bluetooth device.

✓ Turn the Bluetooth device on.

✓ Make sure the Bluetooth device is "discoverable," which means that your computer can see the device. If you are adding a Bluetooth mouse or keyboard, the device may have a button that you can press to make the device discoverable. To determine how to make your Bluetooth device discoverable, refer to the documentation that came with your device.

✓ If you are adding a Bluetooth mouse or keyboard, you must have a mouse or keyboard with a cable connected to your computer.

Before you can use a Bluetooth device, you need to add the device to your computer.

You can obtain many types of Bluetooth devices, such as a mouse, keyboard, cell phone, printer and headset.

ADD A BLUETOOTH DEVICE

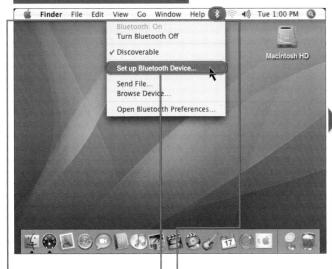

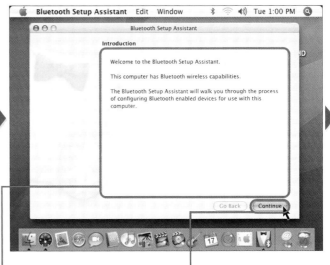

■ In this example, we are adding a Bluetooth headset to a computer.

■ When Bluetooth capability is built-in on your computer or a Bluetooth adapter is attached to your computer, the Bluetooth icon (✳) appears on the menu bar.

1 To add a Bluetooth device to your computer, click the Bluetooth icon (✳). A menu appears.

2 Click **Set up Bluetooth Device**.

■ The Bluetooth Setup Assistant appears.

■ This area states that your computer has Bluetooth wireless capabilities and provides information about the Bluetooth Setup Assistant.

3 Click **Continue** to continue.

CONTINUED

ADD A BLUETOOTH DEVICE

When adding a Bluetooth device to your computer, you may need to enter a passkey for the device.

A passkey enables Mac OS X to identify your Bluetooth device and helps secure the data passing between your computer and the device. Some Bluetooth devices do not use a passkey.

You should refer to the documentation that came with your Bluetooth device to determine if your device requires a specific passkey.

ADD A BLUETOOTH DEVICE (CONTINUED)

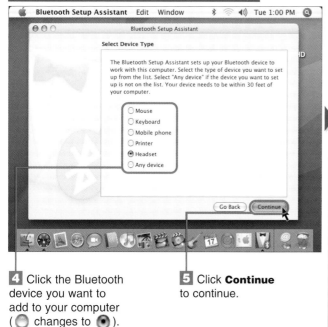

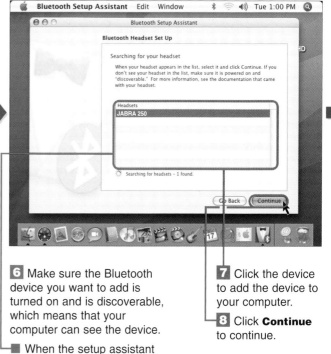

4 Click the Bluetooth device you want to add to your computer (⭕ changes to ⦿).

5 Click **Continue** to continue.

6 Make sure the Bluetooth device you want to add is turned on and is discoverable, which means that your computer can see the device.

■ When the setup assistant finds your Bluetooth device, the device appears in this list.

7 Click the device to add the device to your computer.

8 Click **Continue** to continue.

Tip

Is there a faster way to add a Bluetooth device to my computer?

When a Bluetooth device is turned on, discoverable and in range of your Bluetooth-enabled computer, a dialog box may appear, stating that the Bluetooth device is requesting a pairing with the computer. You can simply enter the passkey for the device into the dialog box and then click **Pair** to quickly add the Bluetooth device to the computer.

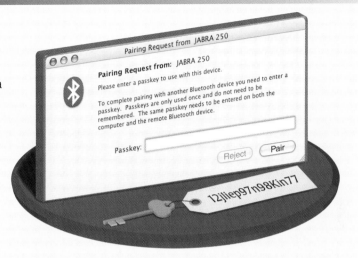

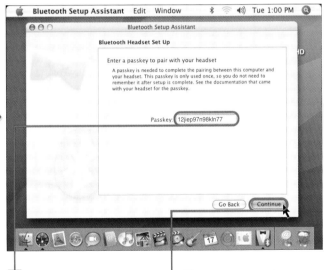

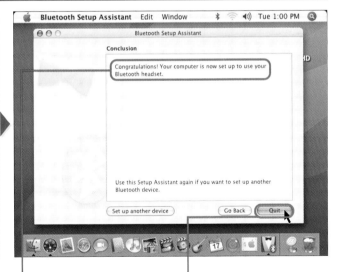

9 Type the passkey for the device.

Note: You can refer to the documentation that came with your Bluetooth device to determine the passkey.

■ If this screen does not appear, your device does not require a passkey. Skip to step **11**.

10 Click **Continue** to continue.

■ This message appears when you have successfully added the Bluetooth device to your computer. Your computer and the device can now communicate whenever the device is within range of your computer.

11 Click **Quit** to close the setup assistant.

Note: Depending on the Bluetooth device you added, you may need to perform other steps to allow the device to communicate with your computer. Refer to the documentation that came with your device to determine what steps, if any, you need to perform.

CHAPTER 5

Using Mac OS X Applications

You can use the applications included with Mac OS X to perform many tasks on your computer. In this chapter, you will learn how to use Mac OS X applications to create documents and electronic sticky notes, track your appointments in an electronic calendar, keep track of your contacts in an address book, and more.

PLAY CHESS

You can play a game of chess on your computer.

When you play a game of chess, the computer is your opponent.

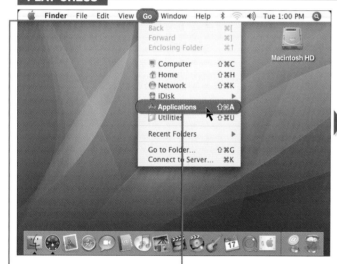

1 Click **Go**.

Note: If Go is not available, click a blank area on your desktop to display the Finder menu bar.

2 Click **Applications** to view the applications available on your computer.

■ The Applications window appears, displaying the applications available on your computer.

3 Double-click **Chess** to play a game of chess.

Note: You can click ⬤ in the Applications window to close the window.

Tip

How can I use spoken commands to play chess?

You must have a microphone connected to your computer to use spoken commands to play chess. To have your computer listen to your spoken commands, press and hold down the esc key as you speak into the microphone. To tell your computer where to move a chess piece, use the numbers and letters along the left and bottom edges of the chessboard, such as "Knight g1 to f3."

Tip

Can I get help with my next chess move?

If you are not sure what your next chess move should be, you can select the **Moves** menu and then click **Show Hint** to have Chess suggest a move. The move Chess suggests will appear as a red arrow on the chessboard.

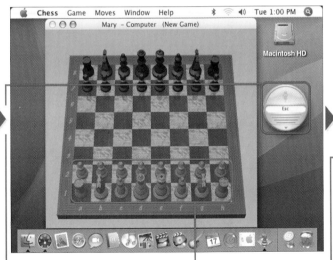

■ The Chess window appears, displaying a three-dimensional chessboard.

■ The Speech Feedback window also appears, allowing you to use spoken commands to play chess.

Note: To use spoken commands to play chess, see the top of this page.

■ To start the game, you must move a chess piece.

4 To move a chess piece, drag the chess piece to a new location on the chessboard.

Note: If you move a chess piece to an invalid location, an alert will sound and the chess piece will return to its original location.

■ After you move a chess piece, the computer will automatically move a chess piece.

5 When you finish playing chess, click **Chess**.

6 Click **Quit Chess** to close the Chess window.

USING ADDRESS BOOK

You can use Address Book to store information for people you frequently contact.

Mail and other applications can use the information in Address Book. For example, when you compose an e-mail message, Mail can quickly fill in the e-mail address of a person you have added to Address Book.

USING ADDRESS BOOK

DISPLAY ADDRESS BOOK

1 Click the Address Book icon to display Address Book.

■ The Address Book window appears.

■ This area displays the groups in Address Book.

Note: To create a group, see page 128.

■ This area displays the people in the highlighted group.

Note: Your name automatically appears in the All group and displays the ♟ symbol.

ADD A PERSON

1 To add a person to Address Book, click the group you want to add the person to. The group is highlighted.

*Note: If you have not added groups to Address Book, select the **All** group.*

2 Click ⊕ to add a new person to Address Book.

Why does a plus sign ( ) appear when I enter information for a person?

A plus sign appears if Address Book can display a related area where you can enter information. To display the related area, click the plus sign (⊕). For example, after you enter a mobile phone number, you can click the plus sign (⊕) beside **mobile** to display an area where you can enter a home phone number.

When entering information for a person, can I change the label for an area?

Yes. You may want to change the label for an area to better describe the information you want to enter in the area. For example, you can change the label "mobile" to "pager."

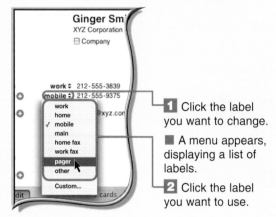

1 Click the label you want to change.

■ A menu appears, displaying a list of labels.

2 Click the label you want to use.

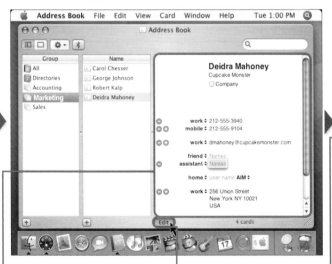

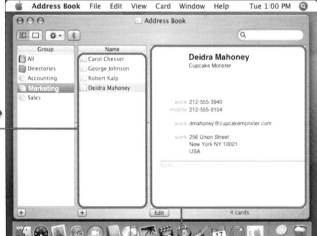

■ Address Book displays areas where you can enter information for the person.

3 Click an area and type the appropriate information for the person. Then press the return key.

4 Repeat step **3** for each area where you want to enter information for the person.

Note: You do not need to enter information into every area.

5 When you finish entering the information for the person, click **Edit** to save the information.

■ The name you entered for the person appears in this area.

■ This area displays the information you entered for the person.

CONTINUED ▶

USING ADDRESS BOOK

You can browse through Address Book to find information for a specific person. You can also edit the information for a person or delete a person you no longer contact.

USING ADDRESS BOOK (CONTINUED)

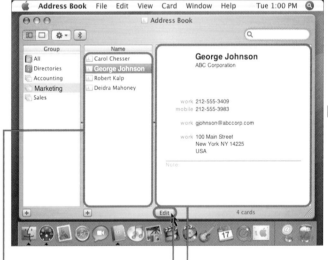

DISPLAY A PERSON'S INFORMATION

1 Click the group that contains a person of interest.

Note: The All group contains all the people you have added to Address Book.

■ This area displays the people in the group you selected.

2 Click the name of a person of interest.

■ This area displays the information for the person.

EDIT A PERSON'S INFORMATION

1 To edit the information for a person, click the name of the person.

■ This area displays the information for the person.

2 Click **Edit** to edit the person's information.

Can I add a picture to a person's information in Address Book?

Yes. Click the name of the person whose information you want to add a picture to. Locate the picture you want to add to the information and then drag the picture into the box beside the person's name in the Address Book window. A window that allows you to crop the picture may appear. Click **Set** to use the picture.

How do I search for a person in Address Book?

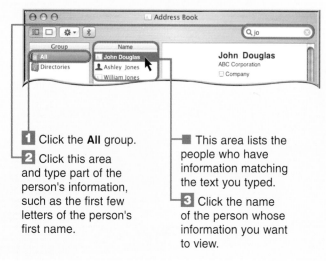

1 Click the **All** group.

2 Click this area and type part of the person's information, such as the first few letters of the person's first name.

■ This area lists the people who have information matching the text you typed.

3 Click the name of the person whose information you want to view.

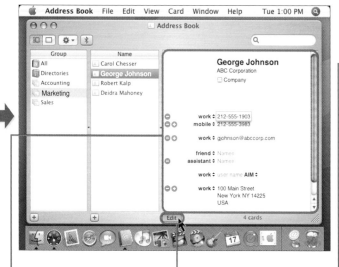

3 Click the information you want to edit. The information is highlighted.

4 Type the new information and then press the return key.

5 Repeat steps **3** and **4** for each area of information you want to edit.

6 Click **Edit** to save your changes.

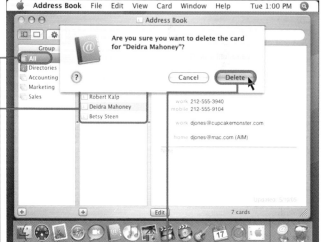

DELETE A PERSON

1 Click **All** to display all the people you have added to Address Book.

2 Click the name of the person you want to remove from Address Book.

3 Press the delete key.

■ A confirmation dialog sheet appears.

4 Click **Delete** to remove the person from Address Book.

CONTINUED

USING ADDRESS BOOK

You can create groups to organize the people in Address Book. For example, you can create groups such as Family, Friends, Clients and Colleagues.

You can create as many groups as you need. A person can belong to more than one group.

Mail and other applications can use a group you create in Address Book. For example, Mail can use a group you added to Address Book to quickly address an e-mail message to each person in the group.

USING ADDRESS BOOK (CONTINUED)

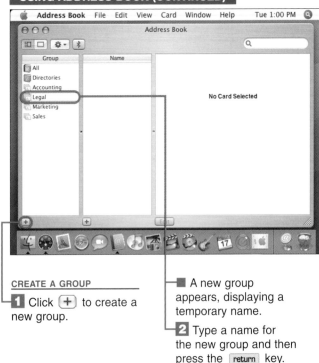

CREATE A GROUP

1 Click ⊕ to create a new group.

■ A new group appears, displaying a temporary name.

2 Type a name for the new group and then press the `return` key.

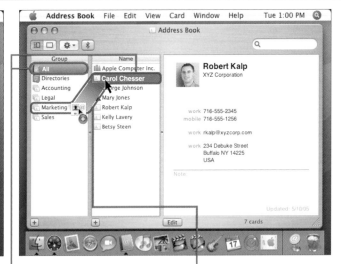

ADD PEOPLE TO A GROUP

1 Click **All** to display all the people you have added to Address Book.

2 Position the mouse ▸ over the person you want to add to a specific group.

3 Drag the person to the group (▸ changes to 📇).

Note: When you drag a person to a group, a box appears around the group.

■ The person's information is copied to the group.

Tip

Can I remove a person from a group?

Yes. Click the group that contains a person you want to remove. Click the name of the person you want to remove from the group and then press the delete key. In the confirmation dialog sheet that appears, click **Remove from Group** to remove the person from the group without removing the person from Address Book.

 Tip

How do I rename a group in Address Book?

Double-click the name of the group you want to rename. A box appears around the name of the group. Type a new name for the group and then press the return key. You cannot rename the All group.

DELETE A GROUP

1 Click the group you want to remove from Address Book.

*Note: You cannot remove the **All** group.*

2 Press the delete key.

Note: Removing a group does not remove the people in the group from Address Book.

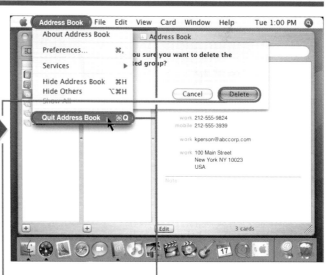

■ A confirmation dialog sheet appears.

3 Click **Delete** to remove the group from Address Book.

QUIT ADDRESS BOOK

1 When you finish using Address Book, click **Address Book**.

2 Click **Quit Address Book**.

USING iCAL

You can use iCal to keep track of your appointments, such as business meetings and lunch dates.

iCal uses the date and time set in your computer to determine today's date. To change the date and time set in your computer, see page 86.

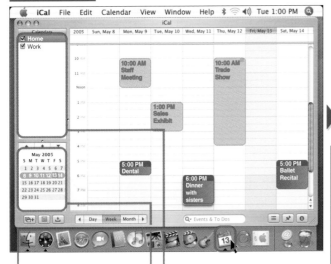

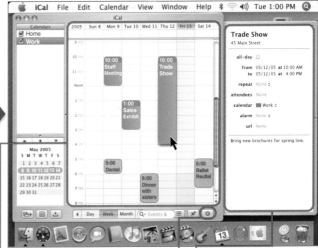

1 Click the iCal icon to start iCal.

■ The iCal window appears.

■ This area displays all your calendars. The box (☑) beside each calendar name shows the color that events in the calendar display.

■ This area displays the days in the current month. The current week is highlighted and the current day is blue.

■ This area displays the events for the current week.

Note: To add an event, see page 132.

2 To display information about an event, double-click the event.

■ This area displays information about the event you selected.

3 To display or hide the information area at any time, click ⓘ.

Tip

Can I search for an event in my calendar?

If you have forgotten the date or time of an event you scheduled, you can search iCal for the event.

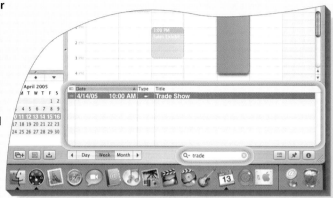

Click the Search area and type a word or phrase in the subject of the event you want to find. iCal displays all the events that contain the word or phrase in the Search Result area. To display an event on the calendar, click the event.

Note: To hide the Search Result area, drag the mouse ⌶ over the text you typed in the Search area and press the `delete` *key.*

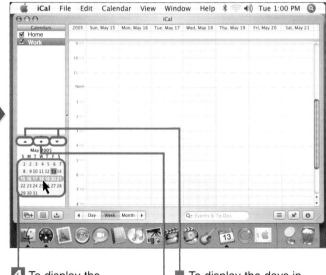

4 To display the events for another week, click a day in the week. The week you select is highlighted.

■ To display the days in another month, click ▲ or ▼ to move backward or forward through the months.

■ To quickly return to the current month, click ◆.

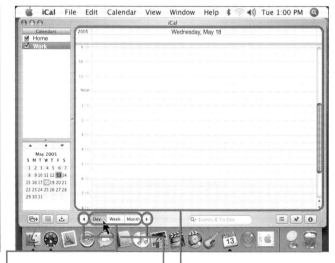

CHANGE THE VIEW OF THE CALENDAR

1 Click an option to specify if you want to display a day, week or month in the iCal window.

■ The iCal window displays the period of time you selected.

■ You can click ◀ or ▶ to display the previous or next day, week or month.

CONTINUED

USING iCAL

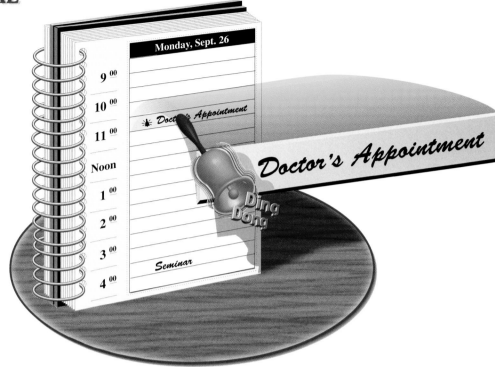

You can add an event to iCal to remind you of an activity, such as a seminar or doctor's appointment.

USING iCAL (CONTINUED)

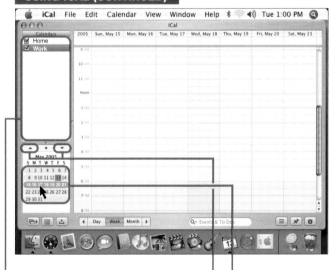

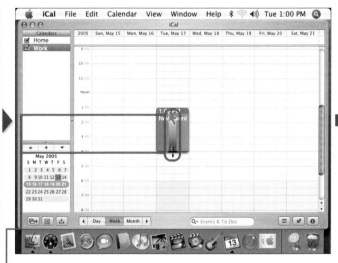

SCHEDULE AN EVENT

1 Click the calendar you want to add an event to.

Note: iCal displays the events for each calendar that displays a check mark (✔). Click the box beside a calendar name to add (☑) or remove (☐) a check mark.

2 Click the day you want to add an event to.

■ To display the days in another month, click ▲ or ▼.

3 Position the mouse ▶ over the starting time for the event.

4 Drag the mouse ┼ to select the amount of time you want to set aside for the event.

5 Type a subject for the event and then press the return key.

Tip

How do I set up an all-day event?

Perform steps **1** to **6** below to schedule an event and display the information area. In the information area, click 🔲 beside all-day (🔲 changes to ☑) to set the event as an all-day event.

 Tip

Can I schedule an event to repeat on a regular basis?

You can schedule an event to repeat at the same time every day or on the same day every week, month or year. Perform steps **1** to **6** below to schedule an event and display the information area. In the information area, click ＄ beside **repeat** to have the event repeat on a regular basis. In the menu that appears, click an option to select the frequency that you want to repeat the event.

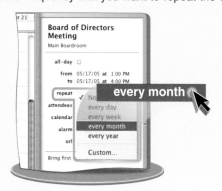

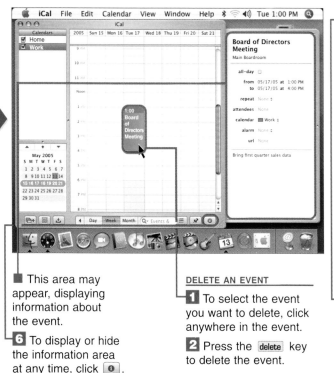

■ This area may appear, displaying information about the event.

6 To display or hide the information area at any time, click 🛈.

DELETE AN EVENT

1 To select the event you want to delete, click anywhere in the event.

2 Press the delete key to delete the event.

QUIT iCAL

1 When you finish using iCal, click **iCal**.

2 Click **Quit iCal**.

USING THE CALCULATOR

You can use the Calculator to perform simple mathematical calculations.

The Calculator allows you to perform the same calculations you would perform on a handheld calculator.

USING THE CALCULATOR

1 Click **Go**.

Note: If Go is not available, click a blank area on your desktop to display the Finder menu bar.

2 Click **Applications** to view the applications available on your computer.

■ The Applications window appears.

3 Double-click **Calculator** to start the Calculator.

■ The Calculator appears.

Note: You can click ⬤ in the Applications window to close the window.

4 To enter information into the Calculator, click each button as you would press the buttons on a handheld calculator.

Note: You can also use the keys on your keyboard to enter information into the Calculator.

Tip

Can I use the Calculator to perform advanced mathematical calculations?

Yes. The Calculator offers a Scientific view, which allows you to perform advanced mathematical and statistical calculations.

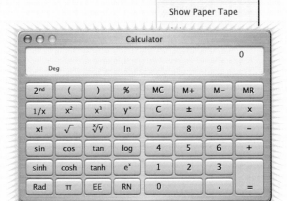

1 Click the **View** menu.

2 Click **Scientific**.

■ The Scientific view of the calculator appears.

■ To return to the Basic view, repeat steps **1** and **2**, selecting **Basic** in step **2**.

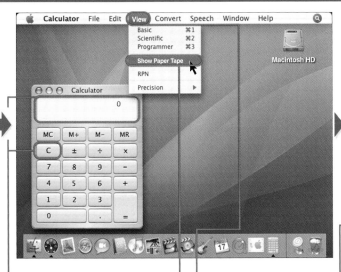

■ This area displays the numbers and operators you enter and the result of each calculation.

■ You can click `C` to start a new calculation at any time.

5 To display the steps for a calculation, click the **View** menu.

6 Click **Show Paper Tape**.

■ The Paper Tape window appears, displaying the numbers and operators you enter and the result of each calculation.

■ You can click **Clear** to clear the paper tape.

7 To close the Paper Tape window, click ⊙ in the window.

8 When you finish using the Calculator, click ⊙ to close the Calculator.

You can use TextEdit to create and edit documents, such as letters and memos.

TextEdit offers only basic word processing features. If you require more advanced features, you may want to obtain a more sophisticated word processor, such as Microsoft Word.

USING TEXTEDIT

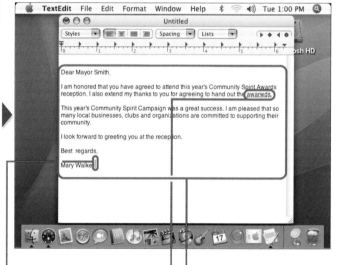

1 Click **Go**.

Note: If Go is not available, click a blank area on your desktop to display the Finder menu bar.

2 Click **Applications** to view the applications available on your computer.

■ The Applications window appears.

3 Double-click **TextEdit** to start TextEdit.

■ A new document window appears.

Note: You can click ⬤ in the Applications window to close the window.

■ The flashing insertion point indicates where the text you type will appear.

4 Type the text for the document.

■ TextEdit checks your spelling as you type and displays a dotted red underline below potential spelling errors. The dotted red underlines will not appear when you print the document.

Can TextEdit help me correct a spelling error in a document?

Yes. To get help correcting a spelling error in a document, press and hold down the [control] key as you click the misspelled word. A menu appears, displaying suggestions to correct the spelling error. Click the suggestion you want to use to correct the spelling error.

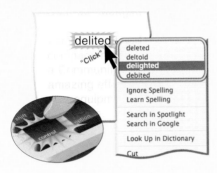

Can I change how TextEdit wraps text?

Yes. By default, TextEdit wraps text based on the width of the document window. To have TextEdit wrap text based on the width of the paper you will print on, select the **Format** menu and then click **Wrap to Page**. Wrapping text to the width of the paper you will print on helps prevent unexpected results when printing a document.

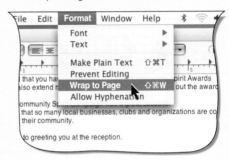

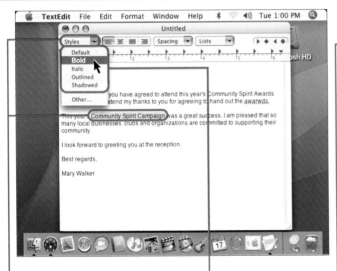

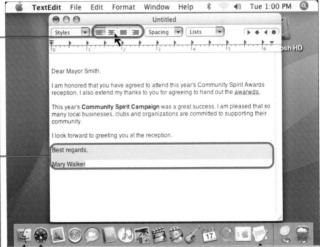

CHANGE TEXT STYLE

1 To select the text you want to change, drag the mouse I over the text until the text is highlighted.

2 Click ▼ in this area to display the available text styles.

3 Click the text style you want to use.

■ The text appears in the new style.

*Note: You can repeat steps 1 to 3, selecting **Default** in step 3 to remove a style from text.*

CHANGE TEXT ALIGNMENT

1 To select the text you want to change, drag the mouse I over the text until the text is highlighted.

2 Click one of these options.

≡ Left align

≡ Center

≡ Justify

≡ Right align

■ The text displays the new alignment.

CONTINUED

137

USING TEXTEDIT

You can change the font of text to enhance the appearance of text.

After you finish creating and making changes to your document, you can save the document.

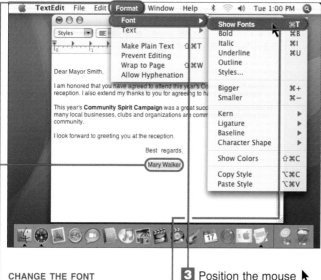

CHANGE THE FONT

1 To select the text you want to change, drag the mouse ⌶ over the text until the text is highlighted.

2 Click **Format**.

3 Position the mouse ▶ over **Font**.

4 Click **Show Fonts**.

■ The Font window appears.

5 Click the font collection containing the font you want to use.

*Note: If you do not know which collection contains the font, click **All Fonts**.*

6 Click the font family you want to use.

7 Click the typeface you want to use.

8 Click the size you want to use.

9 When you finish making changes to the text, click ⬤ to close the Font window.

Tip

Can I change the line spacing of text?

Yes. Changing the line spacing changes the amount of space between lines of text. You can choose from single or double line spacing.

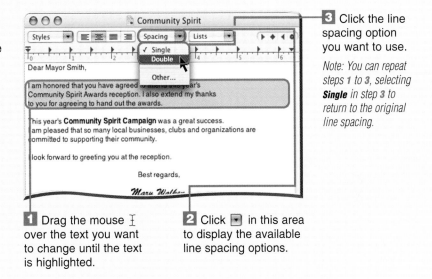

3 Click the line spacing option you want to use.

Note: You can repeat steps 1 to 3, selecting **Single** *in step 3 to return to the original line spacing.*

1 Drag the mouse I over the text you want to change until the text is highlighted.

2 Click ▼ in this area to display the available line spacing options.

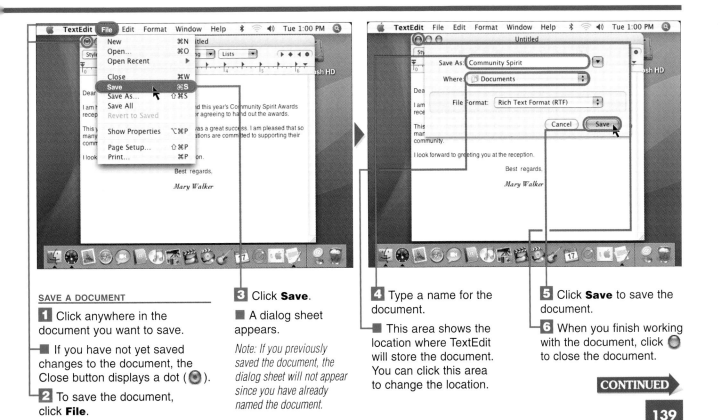

SAVE A DOCUMENT

1 Click anywhere in the document you want to save.

■ If you have not yet saved changes to the document, the Close button displays a dot (●).

2 To save the document, click **File**.

3 Click **Save**.

■ A dialog sheet appears.

Note: If you previously saved the document, the dialog sheet will not appear since you have already named the document.

4 Type a name for the document.

■ This area shows the location where TextEdit will store the document. You can click this area to change the location.

5 Click **Save** to save the document.

6 When you finish working with the document, click ● to close the document.

CONTINUED

USING TEXTEDIT

You can open a saved TextEdit document to display the document on your screen. This allows you to review and make changes to the document.

USING TEXTEDIT (CONTINUED)

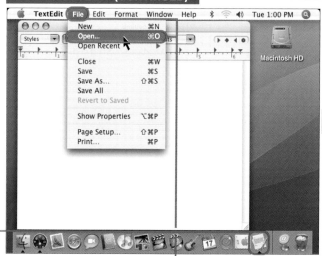

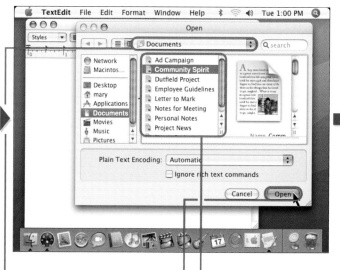

OPEN A DOCUMENT

1 Click the TextEdit icon to make TextEdit the active application.

Note: A new document window may appear.

■ If the TextEdit icon does not appear in the Dock, see page 136 to start the application.

2 Click **File**.

3 Click **Open**.

■ The Open dialog box appears.

■ This area shows the location of the displayed documents. You can click this area to change the location.

4 Click the name of the document you want to open.

5 Click **Open** to open the document.

How do I create a new TextEdit document?

To create a new TextEdit document, select the **File** menu and then click **New**. A new document window will appear on your screen.

Can TextEdit read the text in an open document aloud?

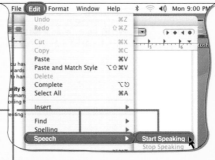

1 To have TextEdit read the text in a document aloud, click **Edit**.

2 Position the mouse over **Speech**.

3 Click **Start Speaking**.

■ TextEdit reads the text in the document aloud.

Note: To stop TextEdit from reading the text in the document aloud, repeat steps 1 to 3, selecting Stop Speaking in step 3.

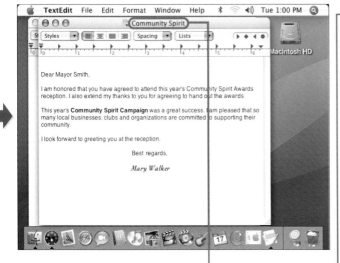

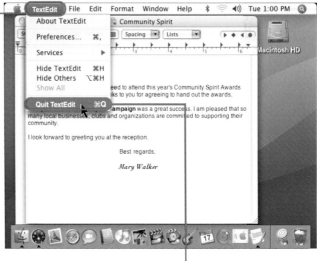

■ The document appears on your screen. You can now review and make changes to the document.

■ This area displays the name of the document.

QUIT TEXTEDIT

1 When you finish using TextEdit, click **TextEdit**.

2 Click **Quit TextEdit**.

USING STICKIES

You can create colorful, electronic notes that are similar to paper sticky notes.

Sticky notes are useful for storing small pieces of information, such as to-do lists, phone numbers, reminders, questions or ideas.

USING STICKIES

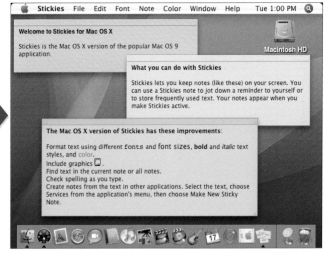

1 Click **Go**.

Note: If Go is not available, click a blank area on your desktop to display the Finder menu bar.

2 Click **Applications** to view the applications available on your computer.

■ The Applications window appears.

3 Double-click **Stickies** to start Stickies.

■ All your notes appear on your screen.

Note: You can click ⊙ in the Applications window to close the window.

■ Stickies comes with several sample notes that describe some of the application's features. To close the sample notes, see page 144.

Can I resize a note?

Yes. Click the note you want to resize. Position the mouse over 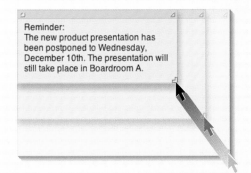 at the bottom right corner of the note and then drag until the note displays the size you want.

How can I quickly reduce the size of a note?

You can quickly collapse a sticky note to view other items on your screen more easily. Double-click the bar at the top of the note you want to collapse. The note collapses to show only the first line of text in the note. To once again display the entire sticky note, double-click the bar again.

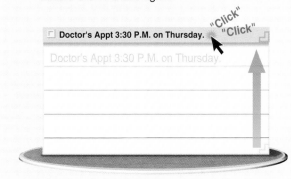

CREATE A NOTE

1 Click **File**.

2 Click **New Note**.

■ A new sticky note appears.

■ The flashing insertion point indicates where the text you type will appear in the note.

3 Type the text for the note.

Note: You do not have to save the notes you create. Each time you open Stickies, the notes you have created will be displayed for you.

CONTINUED ▶

USING STICKIES

You can change the color of a note to help organize the notes. For example, you may want to display work-related notes in green, and personal notes in purple.

When you no longer need a note, you can close the note to remove it from your screen. You can have Stickies save the contents of the note as a text file on your computer or permanently delete the note.

USING STICKIES (CONTINUED)

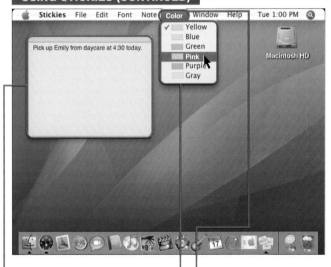

CHANGE THE COLOR OF A NOTE

1 Click the note you want to display a different color.

2 Click **Color** to display a list of the available colors.

3 Click the color you want to use for the note.

■ The note will display the color you selected.

CLOSE A NOTE

1 Click the note you want to close.

2 Click ▢ to close the note.

■ A dialog box appears, asking if you want to save the note.

3 To save the contents of the note as a text file on your computer, click **Save**.

■ To permanently delete the note, click **Don't Save**.

Tip

Can I move a note to a new location on my screen?

Yes. Click the note you want to move and then position the mouse ⊾ over the bar at the top of the note. Drag the note to where you want to place the note on your screen.

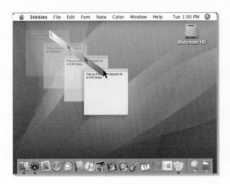

Tip

Can I print a note I have created?

Yes. You can print a note to produce a paper copy of the note. To print a note, click the note you want to print. Click the **File** menu and then click **Print Active Note**. In the dialog box that appears, click **Print** to print the note.

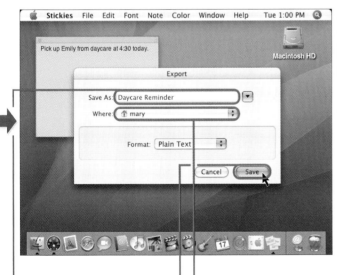

■ The Export dialog box appears, allowing you to save the contents of the note.

4 Type a name for the note.

■ This area shows the location where the note will be saved. You can click this area to change the location.

5 Click **Save** to save the note.

QUIT STICKIES

1 When you finish reviewing and working with your sticky notes, click **Stickies**.

2 Click **Quit Stickies**.

■ When you quit Stickies, all your notes are automatically saved on your computer and will reappear the next time you start Stickies.

USING FONT BOOK

You can use Font Book to view the characters that are available for each font installed on your computer.

Font Book allows you to review the characters a font offers before choosing to use the font in your documents.

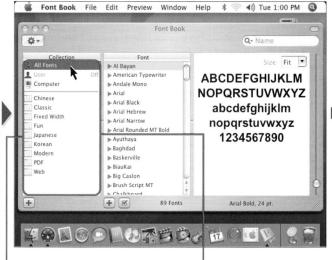

1 Click **Go**.

Note: If Go is not available, click a blank area on your desktop to display the Finder menu bar.

2 Click **Applications** to view the applications available on your computer.

■ The Applications window appears.

3 Double-click **Font Book** to start Font Book.

■ The Font Book window appears.

Note: You can click ⬤ in the Applications window to close the window.

■ This area displays the available font collections on your computer.

4 Click a collection containing the font you want to view.

*Note: If you do not know which collection contains the font you want to view, click **All Fonts**.*

Tip

Can I search for fonts in Font Book?

Yes. You can search Font Book to find a font or font style of interest.

1 Click the **All Fonts** collection to search through all the fonts on your computer.

2 Click this area and then type the font name or style of interest.

■ Font Book displays the names of only the fonts that match the information you specified.

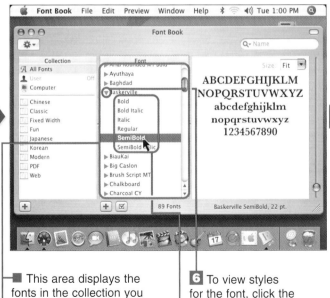

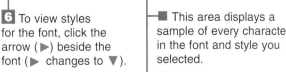

■ This area displays the fonts in the collection you selected.

5 Click the font you want to view.

6 To view styles for the font, click the arrow (▶) beside the font (▶ changes to ▼).

■ A list of styles for the font appears.

7 Click a font style of interest.

■ This area displays a sample of every character in the font and style you selected.

■ You can drag this slider (●) up or down to increase or decrease the size of the displayed characters.

8 To view other fonts of interest, repeat steps **4** to **7**.

9 To quit Font Book, click **Font Book**.

10 Click **Quit Font Book**.

USING DASHBOARD

You can use the Dashboard to access many mini applications, called widgets.

Each widget allows you to perform a specific task. For example, the Dictionary widget allows you to find a definition by typing all or part of a word.

USING DASHBOARD

1 Click the Dashboard icon to start the Dashboard.

Note: You can also press the **F12** *key at any time to start the Dashboard.*

■ Widgets, or mini applications, appear on your screen. By default the Calculator, World Clock, Calendar and Weather widgets are displayed.

■ The Calculator widget allows you to perform basic calculations.

■ The World Clock widget displays the current time in Cupertino, California.

■ The Calendar widget displays the current date and a calendar of the current month.

■ The Weather widget displays the current temperature as well as the five-day forecast for Cupertino, California.

Tip

What widgets does the Dashboard include?

 Address Book   iTunes   Translation

 Calculator   Phone Book   Unit Converter

 Calendar   Stickies   Weather

 Dictionary   Stocks   World Clock

 Flight Tracker   Tile Game

■ You can work with the widgets on your screen or customize the widgets to suit your needs.

2 To customize a widget, move the mouse over the widget.

■ If the widget is customizable, *i* appears on the widget.

3 Click *i* to customize the widget.

Note: In this example, we customize the World Clock widget to display the time for another location in the world.

■ Areas appear, allowing you to customize the widget.

4 This area displays the current continent. Click this area to select a different continent that you want to display the time for.

5 This area displays the current city the World Clock displays the time for. Click this area to select a different city that you want to display the time for.

6 Click **Done** to have the World Clock display the time for the city you selected.

CONTINUED

USING DASHBOARD

Mac OS X provides many widgets that you can use. You can display widgets on your screen that you find useful. Each time you start the Dashboard, the widgets you have previously displayed will reappear on your screen.

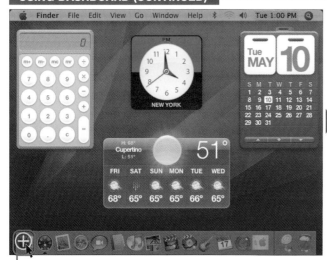

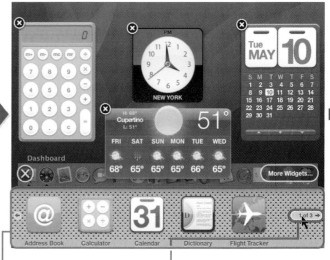

7 To display other widgets that you can use, click ⊕.

■ A row of widgets you can use appears.

■ When you position the mouse ▶ over this area, the area displays the number of the current row of widgets you are viewing and the total number of rows of widgets.

8 To view the next row of widgets, click this area.

How can I obtain more widgets?

Perform step **7** below and then click **More Widgets**. A Web browser window opens, displaying a Web page offering more widgets that you can download to your computer. Follow the instructions on the Web page to download more widgets.

 How can I remove a widget I no longer use from my screen?

When you display the Dashboard, you can remove a widget you no longer use from your screen.

1 When working with the Dashboard, click ⊕.

2 A close button (⊗) appears at the top left corner of each widget on your screen. To remove a widget from your screen, click ⊗.

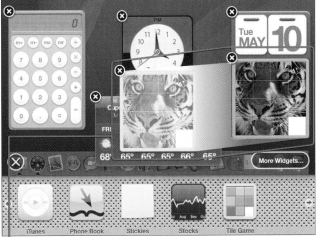

■ A new row of widgets you can use appears.

9 To use a widget in the row, click the widget.

■ The widget appears on your screen.

10 To move a widget to a new location on your screen, position the mouse ▶ over an edge of the widget and drag the widget to a new location.

11 To close the Dashboard and redisplay the Mac OS X desktop, press the F12 key.

■ When you close the Dashboard, all your widgets and their locations on the screen are automatically saved and will reappear the next time you start the Dashboard.

CHAPTER 6

Work With Songs and Videos

In this chapter, you will learn how to use the iTunes program to play music CDs and listen to radio stations that broadcast on the Internet. You will also learn how to copy songs to a CD or an iPod, play QuickTime and DVD movies, and much more.

LISTEN TO A MUSIC CD

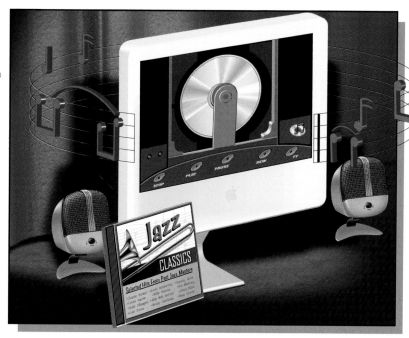

You can use the iTunes application to listen to music CDs on your computer while you work.

The first time you start iTunes, a license agreement appears on your screen. Click **Agree** to continue. The iTunes Setup Assistant then appears. Follow the instructions on your screen to set up iTunes.

LISTEN TO A MUSIC CD

1 Insert a music CD into your computer's CD drive.

■ After a moment, the iTunes window appears.

2 Click the name of the CD in this area.

*Note: If the name of the CD is not displayed, click **Audio CD**.*

3 Click ▶ to start playing the CD.

■ This area lists the songs on the CD and the amount of time each song will play. The song that is currently playing displays a speaker icon (◀🔊).

■ To play a specific song in the list, double-click the name of the song.

■ iTunes will play each song that displays a check mark. To add (✔) or remove (☐) a check mark for a song, click the box (☐) beside the song.

Tip

How does iTunes know the name of each song on my music CD?

If you are connected to the Internet when you insert a music CD, iTunes attempts to obtain information about the CD, such as the track names, from the Internet. If you are not connected to the Internet or information about the CD is unavailable, iTunes displays the track number of each song instead. If iTunes is able to obtain information about the CD, iTunes will recognize the CD and display the appropriate information each time you insert the CD.

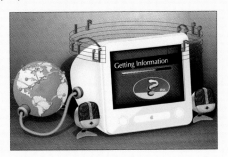

 Tip

Can I play the songs on my music CD in random order?

Yes. You can shuffle the songs to play the songs in random order. Click ⤨ in the iTunes window to shuffle the songs. To once again play the songs on the CD in order, click ⤨ .

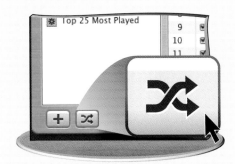

■ This area displays the name of the song that is currently playing and the amount of time the song has been playing.

4 To decrease or increase the volume, drag this slider (◉) left or right.

5 To pause the play of the CD, click ⏸ (⏸ changes to ▶).

Note: You can click ▶ to resume the play of the CD.

6 When you finish listening to the CD, click ⏏ to eject the CD.

7 When you finish listening to CDs, click **iTunes**.

8 Click **Quit iTunes**.

COPY SONGS FROM A MUSIC CD

You can copy songs from your favorite music CD onto your computer.

Copying songs from a music CD, also known as "ripping" music, allows you to play the songs at any time without having to insert the CD into your computer.

The first time you start iTunes, a license agreement appears on your screen. Click **Agree** to continue. The iTunes Setup Assistant then appears. Follow the instructions on your screen to set up iTunes.

COPY SONGS FROM A MUSIC CD

1 Insert a music CD into your computer's CD drive.

■ After a moment, the iTunes window appears.

2 Click the name of the CD in this area.

Note: If the name of the CD is not displayed, click **Audio CD**.

■ This area lists the songs on the CD and the amount of time each song will play.

Note: For information on how iTunes determines the name of each song on a CD, see the top of page 155.

■ iTunes will copy each song that displays a check mark. To add (☑) or remove (☐) a check mark for a song, click the box (☐) beside the song.

3 Click ⊙ to copy the songs to your computer.

Tip

How can I play a song I copied from a music CD?

Tiger offers two ways that you can play a song
you copied from a music CD.

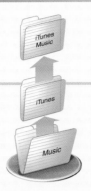

Use the Library

Songs you copy from a music CD are
listed in the iTunes Library. You can click
Library in the iTunes window to display
all the songs in the Library. To play a
song in the Library, see page 158.

Use the iTunes Music folder

Songs you copy from a music CD are stored in the
iTunes Music folder. To view the contents of the iTunes
Music folder, display the contents of the Music folder
(see page 34), double-click the iTunes folder and then
double-click the iTunes Music folder. The iTunes Music
folder contains a folder for each artist whose songs
you have copied. You can double-click a song you
copied from a CD to open iTunes and play the song.

■ iTunes begins
playing the first song
you selected to copy.

■ This area displays
the name of the song
that iTunes is currently
copying and the amount
of time remaining to
complete the copy.

■ The song that iTunes
is currently copying
displays the ⊘ symbol.
Each song that iTunes
has finished copying
displays the ⊘ symbol.

■ To stop the copy at
any time, click ⊗.

■ When iTunes has
finished copying songs
from the CD, a sound
plays. iTunes will
continue to play the
songs you selected
to copy.

4 To eject the CD,
click ⏏.

5 When you finish
copying songs from
a music CD, click
iTunes.

6 Click **Quit iTunes**.

USING THE iTUNES LIBRARY

The Library in iTunes acts like an electronic jukebox, providing a central location where you can view and play songs on your computer.

The first time you start iTunes, a license agreement appears on your screen. Click **Agree** to continue. The iTunes Setup Assistant then appears. Follow the instructions on your screen to set up iTunes.

USING THE iTUNES LIBRARY

1 Click the iTunes icon to start iTunes.

■ The iTunes window appears.

2 Click **Library** to view all the songs in the Library.

■ This area lists all the songs in the Library.

Note: When you first started and set up iTunes, you may have selected to have iTunes automatically add existing songs on your computer to the Library.

ADD A SONG TO THE LIBRARY

1 Locate the song on your computer that you want to add to the Library.

2 Position the mouse ► over the song.

3 Drag the song to the list of songs in the Library (► changes to ⊕).

■ iTunes adds the song to the Library.

Tip

Are there other ways to add songs to the iTunes Library?

Yes. When you double-click a song on your computer that plays in iTunes, iTunes automatically adds the song to the Library. Songs you copy from a music CD are also automatically added to the Library. To copy songs from a music CD, see page 156. To quickly add all the songs in a folder to the Library, position the mouse ⬉ over the folder and then drag the folder to the list of songs in the Library.

Tip

How can I remove a song from the iTunes Library?

To remove a song from the Library, click the song and then press the `delete` key. In the confirmation dialog box that appears, click **Yes** to remove the song. An additional dialog box may appear, asking if you want to remove the song from the iTunes Music folder. Click **Yes** or **No** to specify if you want to remove the song from this folder.

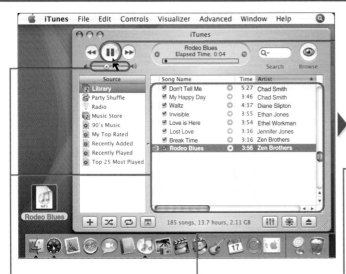

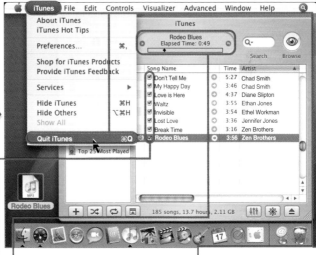

PLAY SONGS IN THE LIBRARY

1 Double-click the name of the song you want to play.

2 To decrease or increase the volume, drag this slider (●) left or right.

Note: To quickly turn off the sound, click ◀). To quickly turn the volume to full capacity, click ◀))).

3 To pause the play of the song, click (⏸) (⏸ changes to ▶).

■ You can click ▶ to resume the play of the song.

■ This area displays the name of the song that is currently playing and the amount of time the song has been playing.

■ When a song finishes playing, iTunes will automatically play the next song in the list that displays a check mark. To add (☑) or remove (☐) a check mark for a song, click the box beside the song.

4 When you finish playing songs in iTunes, click **iTunes**.

5 Click **Quit iTunes**.

159

CREATE A PLAYLIST

You can create personalized lists of your favorite songs, called playlists.

Creating a playlist is useful when you want to listen to a specific group of songs. You can select a playlist and iTunes will play all the songs in the playlist. For example, you can create and play a playlist that contains all your favorite rock songs.

CREATE A PLAYLIST

1 Click the iTunes icon to start iTunes.

■ The iTunes window appears.

2 Click ⊞ to create a new playlist.

■ A new, untitled playlist appears. Playlists display the ♪ symbol.

3 Type a name for the new playlist and then press the `return` key.

4 To add a song to the playlist, click **Library** to view all the songs in the Library.

■ This area lists all the songs in the Library.

Note: For information on the Library, see page 158.

Tip

Can iTunes automatically create playlists for me?

Yes. iTunes automatically creates five Smart
Playlists for you. Smart Playlists are updated
each time you add songs to the iTunes Library.
You can play the songs in a Smart Playlist as you
would play the songs in a playlist you created.

Smart Playlist:	Contains:
90's Music	Songs recorded between 1990 and 1999.
My Top Rated	Songs rated higher than 3 stars.
Recently Added	Songs added to the Library in the past 2 weeks.
Recently Played	Songs played in the past 2 weeks.
Top 25 Most Played	The 25 songs you have played most often.

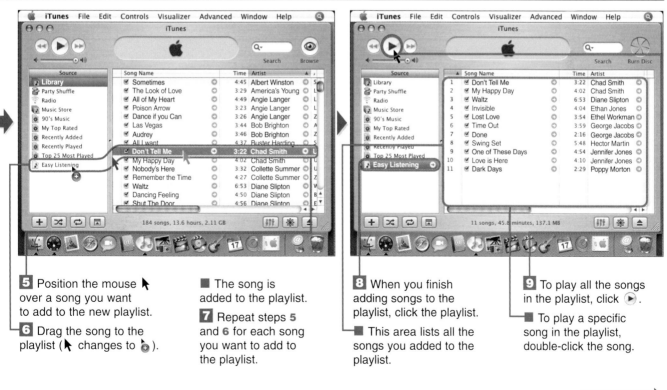

5 Position the mouse ▶ over a song you want to add to the new playlist.

6 Drag the song to the playlist (▶ changes to ⊕).

■ The song is added to the playlist.

7 Repeat steps **5** and **6** for each song you want to add to the playlist.

8 When you finish adding songs to the playlist, click the playlist.

■ This area lists all the songs you added to the playlist.

9 To play all the songs in the playlist, click ▶.

■ To play a specific song in the playlist, double-click the song.

CONTINUED ▶

CREATE A PLAYLIST

After you create a playlist, you can change the order of the songs in the playlist to suit yourself.

You can delete a playlist you no longer need. When you delete a playlist, the songs in the playlist remain in the iTunes Library.

CREATE A PLAYLIST (CONTINUED)

CHANGE THE ORDER OF SONGS

1 To change the order of the songs in the playlist, position the mouse ▶ over a song you want to move to a new location.

2 Drag the song to a new location in the playlist.

■ A black line indicates where the song will appear.

■ The song appears in a new location in the playlist.

3 Repeat steps **1** and **2** for each song you want to move to a new location in the playlist.

Tip

What is the Party Shuffle?

The Party Shuffle is a constantly changing playlist that iTunes creates by randomly choosing songs from the Library.

1 Click **Party Shuffle**.

Note: A dialog box may appear, describing Party Shuffle. Click OK to close the dialog box.

■ A random list of songs from the Library appears.

Note: By default, the list will display the 5 most recently played songs and the next 15 upcoming songs.

2 To play the songs in the Party Shuffle list, click ▶.

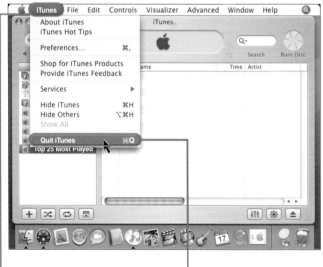

DELETE A PLAYLIST

1 To delete a playlist, click the icon for the playlist you want to delete.

2 Press the delete key.

■ A confirmation dialog box appears.

3 Click **Yes** to delete the playlist.

Note: Deleting a playlist will not remove the songs in the playlist from the Library.

QUIT iTUNES

1 When you finish working with your playlists, click **iTunes**.

2 Click **Quit iTunes**.

CREATE YOUR OWN MUSIC CDS

You can copy songs on your computer to a CD. Copying songs to a CD is also known as "burning" a CD.

You need a computer with a recordable CD drive to create your own music CDs. A CD can typically store about 74 minutes of audio, which is about 20 songs.

CREATE YOUR OWN MUSIC CDS

■ Before you can create your own music CD, you must create a playlist that contains all the songs you want to include on the CD. To create a playlist, see page 160.

1 Click the iTunes icon to start iTunes.

■ The iTunes window appears.

2 Click the playlist that contains the songs you want to copy to a recordable CD.

■ This area lists the songs in the playlist.

3 iTunes will copy each song that displays a check mark. To add (☑) or remove (☐) a check mark for a song, click the box beside the song.

4 To copy the songs you selected to a recordable CD, click ◉ (◉ changes to ◉).

What type of CD should I use to create my music CD?

You should use a CD-R (Compact Disc-Recordable) to create your music CD. Most CD players can play CD-Rs. You cannot erase or change the contents of a CD-R.

If your computer has a CD-RW drive, you can also use a CD-RW (Compact Disc-ReWritable) to create your music CD, but CD-RWs may not play in some CD players. You can erase the contents of a CD-RW in order to copy new music to the disc.

Can I stop iTunes from copying songs to a CD?

Yes. To stop iTunes from copying songs, click ⊗ in the iTunes window. In the confirmation dialog box that appears, click **Yes** to stop the copy. If you are copying songs to a CD-R, keep in mind that you can record data to a CD-R only once.

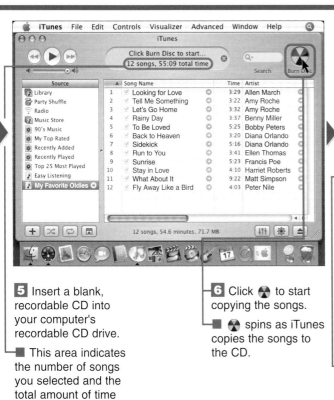

5 Insert a blank, recordable CD into your computer's recordable CD drive.

■ This area indicates the number of songs you selected and the total amount of time the songs will play.

6 Click ● to start copying the songs.

■ ● spins as iTunes copies the songs to the CD.

■ When the copy is complete, the CD appears in this area, displaying the same name as the playlist.

■ This area lists the songs on the CD.

7 Click ▲ to eject the CD.

8 To quit iTunes, click **iTunes**.

9 Click **Quit iTunes**.

COPY SONGS TO AN iPOD

You can use iTunes to copy songs on your computer to an iPod, which is a portable music player.

You can copy songs that you have saved from a music CD or downloaded from the Internet to your iPod.

COPY SONGS TO AN iPOD

■ Before copying songs to an iPod, you may want to create a playlist that contains the songs you want to copy to the iPod. To create a playlist, see page 160.

1 Connect your iPod to your computer and turn on the iPod, if necessary.

■ iTunes opens automatically, displaying the contents of the iTunes Library.

■ The name of your iPod appears in this area.

2 Click the name of your iPod.

■ This area displays the contents of your iPod.

■ This area displays the iTunes location or playlist containing the songs that will be copied to your iPod. You can click this area to select a different location or playlist.

■ If this area does not appear, iTunes will automatically copy all the songs in the Library to your iPod. Skip to step **4**.

Tip

Can I use iTunes to remove a song from my iPod?

To use iTunes to remove a song from your iPod without removing the song from a playlist, perform steps **1** and **2** below to display the contents of your iPod in the iTunes window. Click the song you want to remove and then press the delete key. In the confirmation dialog box that appears, click **Yes** to remove the song from your iPod.

Tip

Can I copy only specific songs to my iPod?

If you do not want to update your iPod with all the contents of a playlist you created, you can copy only specific songs you choose. Perform step **1** below and then click **Library** to display the songs in the iTunes Library. Position your mouse over the name of a song you want to copy to your iPod and then drag the song to the name of your iPod to copy the song.

3 Click **Autofill** to copy the songs to your iPod.

■ While iTunes copies the songs to your iPod, this area displays the progress of the copy.

■ Do not disconnect your iPod from your computer while songs are being copied to the iPod.

■ When the copy is complete, this area displays the amount of free and used space on your iPod.

4 When you finish copying songs to your iPod, click **iTunes**.

5 Click **Quit iTunes**.

LISTEN TO RADIO STATIONS ON THE INTERNET

When you are connected to the Internet, you can listen to radio stations from around the world that broadcast on the Internet.

The first time you start iTunes, a license agreement appears on your screen. Click **Agree** to continue. The iTunes Setup Assistant then appears. Follow the instructions on your screen to set up iTunes.

LISTEN TO RADIO STATIONS ON THE INTERNET

1 Click the iTunes icon to start iTunes.

■ The iTunes window appears.

2 Click **Radio** to listen to radio stations that broadcast on the Internet.

■ This area lists the categories of available radio stations.

3 To display the radio stations in a category, click ▶ beside the category (▶ changes to ▼).

■ The name, bit rate and description of each radio station in the category appear.

Note: The higher the bit rate, the better the sound quality.

■ You can click ▼ beside a category to once again hide the radio stations in the category (▼ changes to ▶).

4 Double-click the radio station you want to play.

Note: If you use a modem to connect to the Internet, you should select a radio station with a bit rate of less than 56 kbps for the best results.

Tip

How can I reduce the size of the iTunes window?

You can reduce the size of the iTunes window so you can easily view other items on your screen while listening to a radio station. Click ⊖ in the top left corner of the iTunes window to reduce the size of the window. To return the iTunes window to its previous size, click ⊖ again.

 Tip

Can I use iTunes to purchase music from the Internet?

Yes. iTunes allows you to connect to Apple's Music Store and purchase songs or entire albums that you can store in your iTunes Library.

■ To use the Music Store to purchase music, click **Music Store** in the iTunes window and then follow the instructions on your screen.

Note: The Music Store is not available in all countries.

■ The radio station begins to play. The selected radio station displays a speaker icon (🔊).

■ This area displays information about the currently playing radio station and the amount of time the radio station has been playing.

5 To decrease or increase the volume, drag this slider (🔘) left or right.

6 To stop playing the radio station, click (⏹) (⏹ changes to ▶).

Note: You can click ▶ to resume the play of the radio station.

■ To play another radio station, double-click the radio station you want to play.

7 When you finish listening to radio stations on the Internet, click **iTunes**.

8 Click **Quit iTunes**.

You can use QuickTime Player to play QuickTime movies on your computer.

You can play QuickTime movies you obtained on the Internet or created using iMovie. For information on using iMovie, see pages 196 to 211.

PLAY QUICKTIME MOVIES

1 Double-click the QuickTime movie you want to play. QuickTime movies display the icon and .mov extension.

■ A QuickTime Player window opens.

Note: The first time you play a QuickTime movie, a dialog box appears, allowing you to purchase QuickTime Pro, an advanced version of QuickTime. You can click an option in the dialog box to continue.

2 Click ▶ to start playing the movie (▶ changes to ❚❚).

■ The movie plays in this area.

■ This area displays the amount of time the movie has been playing and a slider (▼) that indicates the progress of the movie.

3 To decrease or increase the volume, drag this slider (◉) left or right.

Note: To quickly turn off the sound, click ◀)) (◀)) changes to ◀). To once again turn on the sound, click ◀.

Tip

Is there another way to play a QuickTime movie?

Yes. You can find QuickTime movies on the Web that you can play in your Web browser. For example, the www.apple.com/trailers and www.comingsoon.net/trailers Web sites offer QuickTime movies that you can play. When the movie is playing, you can click ▯▯ to pause the movie (▯▯ changes to ▶). To once again play the movie, click ▶.

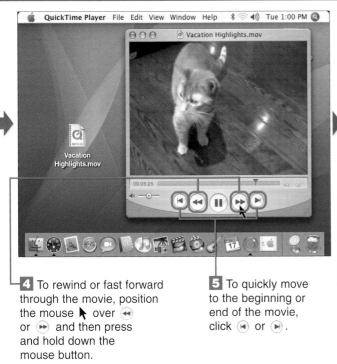

4 To rewind or fast forward through the movie, position the mouse ▶ over ◀◀ or ▶▶ and then press and hold down the mouse button.

5 To quickly move to the beginning or end of the movie, click ◀ or ▶.

6 To pause the play of the movie, click ▯▯ (▯▯ changes to ▶).

■ You can click ▶ to resume the play of the movie.

7 When you finish playing the movie, click **QuickTime Player**.

8 Click **Quit QuickTime Player**.

PLAY A DVD MOVIE

You can use DVD Player to play DVD movies on your computer.

If you have a notebook computer, using your computer to play DVD movies can be especially useful when traveling.

Your computer must have an internal DVD drive to play DVD movies. You can usually play DVD movies only on a computer with an Apple DVD drive.

PLAY A DVD MOVIE

■1 Insert the DVD movie you want to play into your computer's DVD drive.

■ DVD Player starts and the movie automatically begins to play.

■ You can use the playback controller to control the movie.

Note: If the playback controller does not appear, move the mouse on your desk to display the controller.

■ Most DVD movies display a main menu that lists options you can select to play the movie or access special features.

■2 To select an option in the menu, click an arrow in this area to move through the options until you highlight the option you want to select.

■3 Click (enter) to select the highlighted option.

Note: You can also select an option by clicking the option on your screen.

■ To return to this menu at any time, click (menu).

Can I play a DVD movie in a window?

Yes. To play a DVD movie in a window, press and hold down the ⌘ key as you press the `1` (half size), `2` (normal size) or `3` (maximum size) key. To once again play the movie using the entire screen, press and hold down the ⌘ key as you press the `0` key.

Does DVD Player offer any additional features that I can use while viewing a movie?

DVD Player allows you to perform several tasks while viewing a movie, such as viewing a movie in slow motion or displaying subtitles. The additional features may not work for some DVD movies.

■ A drawer displays a button for each feature you can use. Position the mouse ▸ over a button to display the name of the feature.

■ To display or hide the drawer at any time, double-click this area.

4 To increase or decrease the volume of the movie, drag this slider (◉) up or down.

5 To rewind or fast forward through the movie, position the mouse ▸ over ⏪ or ⏩ and then press and hold down the mouse button.

6 To pause the play of the movie, click ⏸ (⏸ changes to ▶).

■ You can click ▶ to resume playing the movie.

7 To stop playing the movie at any time, click ⏹ .

8 To eject the DVD when you finish playing the movie, click `eject` .

9 To quit DVD Player, move the mouse ▸ over the top of the screen and then click **DVD Player** on the menu bar that appears.

10 Click **Quit DVD Player**.

Scuba Diving in the Bahamas

The Annual Regatta

CHAPTER 7

Manage Photos

This chapter teaches you how to use iPhoto to copy photos from a digital camera to your computer so you can view, organize and edit the photos.

Summer Vacation

COPY PHOTOS FROM A DIGITAL CAMERA

You can copy photos from a digital camera to your computer so you can view, organize and edit the photos.

Before you start copying photos, make sure the digital camera is connected to your computer and is turned on. You may also need to set the camera to a specific mode, such as the Connect mode.

COPY PHOTOS FROM A DIGITAL CAMERA

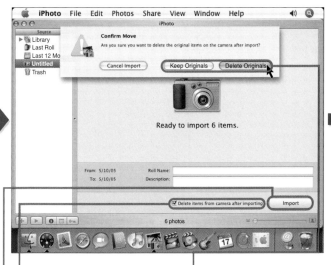

1 Click the iPhoto icon to start iPhoto.

■ The iPhoto window appears.

*Note: The first time you connect your digital camera to your computer, a dialog box appears, asking if you want iPhoto to open automatically when you attach a camera to your computer. Click **Use iPhoto** to have iPhoto open automatically. If iPhoto starts automatically, skip step 1.*

■ This area displays the number of photos stored on the camera.

2 This option will erase the photos on the camera after the photos are copied to your computer. You can click the option to turn the option on (☑) or off (☐).

3 Click **Import** to start copying the photos to your computer.

■ If you selected to erase the photos in step 2, a confirmation dialog sheet appears.

4 Click an option to keep or delete the photos on the camera after the copy is complete.

Tip

How do I delete a photo I copied from my digital camera?

To delete a photo, click **Library** to view all your photos. Click the photo you want to delete and then press the `delete` key. iPhoto will remove the photo from your photo library and from any albums that contain the photo. For information on albums, see page 178. Photos you delete from your photo library are placed in iPhoto's Trash. You must empty iPhoto's Trash to permanently remove the photos.

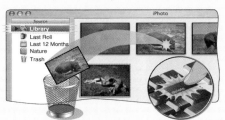

Tip

How do I empty iPhoto's Trash?

Click **Trash** in the top left corner of the iPhoto window to view the photos you have deleted. To permanently remove the photos, click the **iPhoto** menu and then click **Empty Trash**. In the confirmation dialog sheet that appears, click **OK** to permanently delete the photos.

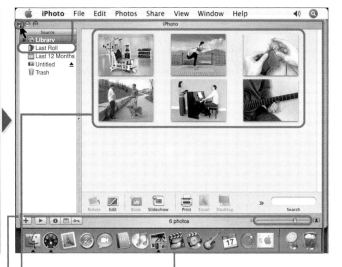

■ This area shows the photo that iPhoto is currently copying.

■ This area shows the progress of the copy.

■ You can click **Stop Import** to stop copying the photos at any time.

■ When the copy is complete, the photos appear in your photo library. The photo library contains all the photos you have copied to your computer.

5 To decrease or increase the size of the photos, drag this slider (⬤) left or right.

■ To quickly display only the last photos you copied from your digital camera, click **Last Roll**.

6 When you finish working with iPhoto, click ⬤ to close the iPhoto window.

CREATE AN ALBUM

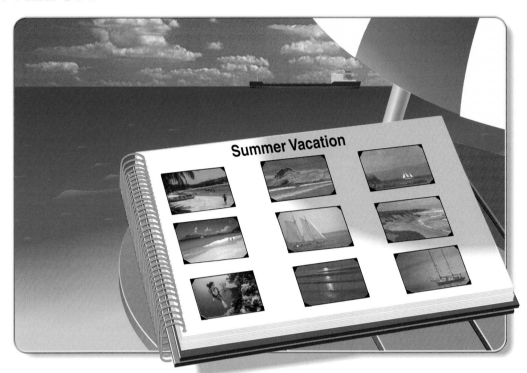

You can create an album that contains photos you want to keep together.

You can create as many albums as you want. For example, you can create an album that contains pictures of your summer vacation and another album that contains pictures of your pet.

CREATE AN ALBUM

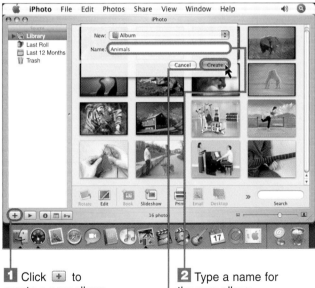

1 Click ⊞ to create a new album.

■ A dialog sheet appears.

2 Type a name for the new album.

3 Click **Create** to create the album.

■ The album appears in this area. Albums display the 🔲 symbol.

4 To add a photo to the album, click **Library** to view all the photos in your photo library.

■ This area displays all the photos in your photo library.

Tip

Can I change the order of photos in an album?

Yes. Click the name of the album that contains the photos you want to reorder. Position the mouse ▸ over a photo you want to move and then drag the photo to a new location in the album. A black line indicates where the photo will appear.

Tip

How do I delete an album?

To delete an album, click the name of the album you want to delete and then press the delete key. In the confirmation dialog sheet that appears, click **Delete** to delete the album. Deleting an album will not remove the photos in the album from your photo library.

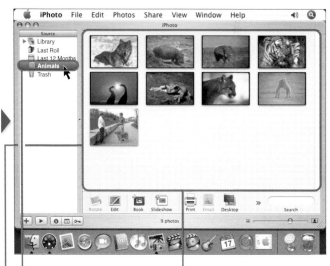

5 Position the mouse ▸ over a photo you want to add to the album.

6 Drag the photo to the album (▸ changes to ⊕).

■ The photo is added to the album.

7 You can repeat steps **5** and **6** for each photo you want to add to the album.

8 When you finish adding photos to the album, click the album.

■ This area displays all the photos you added to the album.

■ If you no longer want a photo to appear in the album, you can click the photo and then press the delete key to delete the photo.

Note: Deleting a photo from an album will not remove the photo from your photo library.

EDIT A PHOTO

You can edit a photo to improve its appearance. For example, you can crop a photo to remove parts of the photo you do not want to show.

Editing a photo will change the appearance of the photo in your photo library and in every album that contains the photo.

EDIT A PHOTO

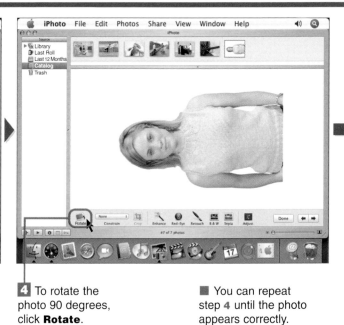

1 Click the album that contains the photos you want to edit. You can also click Library to view all your photos.

2 Click the photo you want to change.

3 Click **Edit** to edit the photo.

4 To rotate the photo 90 degrees, click **Rotate**.

■ You can repeat step 4 until the photo appears correctly.

Tip

Can I make a copy of a photo?

Yes. Making a copy of a photo before you begin editing the photo is useful if you want to edit the photo without changing the original photo. To make a copy of a photo, perform steps **1** to **2** below and then press and hold down the ⌘ key as you press the **D** key. If you make a copy of a photo in an album, iPhoto will also add a copy of the photo to your photo library.

Tip

Can I change a photo back to its original appearance?

If you do not like the changes you made to a photo, you can change the photo back to its original appearance. Select the photo you want to change back to its original appearance. Click the **Photos** menu and then select **Revert to Original**. In the dialog box that appears, click **OK**.

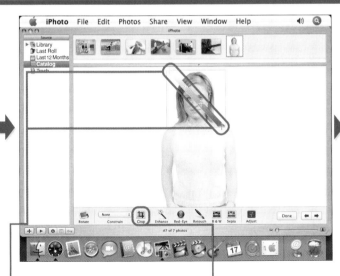

5 To remove parts of the photo you do not want to show, position the mouse ╬ over a corner of the area of the photo you want to show.

6 Drag the mouse ╬ over the photo until you select the entire area you want to show.

7 Click **Crop** to crop the photo and show only the area you selected.

8 To have iPhoto automatically enhance the colors and clarity of the photo, click **Enhance**.

■ The photo displays the enhanced colors and clarity.

CONTINUED ▶

You can use iPhoto's editing features to reduce red-eye and remove small marks or blemishes in your photos.

You can also use iPhoto to convert your photos to black-and-white or sepia images.

EDIT A PHOTO (CONTINUED)

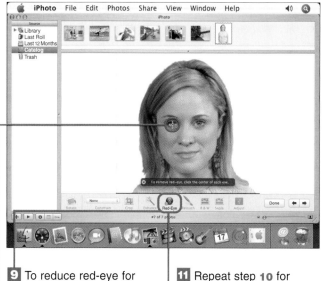

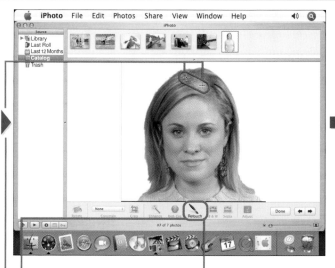

9 To reduce red-eye for a person, click **Red-Eye**.

10 Position the mouse ✛ over the center of the person's eye and then click the mouse button.

11 Repeat step **10** for the person's other eye.

12 When you finish removing shades of red from the person's eyes, click **Red-Eye** again.

13 To retouch a small area in the photo, click **Retouch**.

14 Position the mouse ✛ over the area of the photo you want to retouch.

15 Drag the mouse ✛ away from the area using a short stroke.

16 Repeat step **15** until the area is completely retouched.

17 When you finish retouching the photo, click **Retouch** again.

Tip

Can I undo a change I made without losing all of my changes?

To immediately reverse the last change you made to a photo, click the **Edit** menu and then select **Undo**. The name of the Undo command depends on the last change you made. You can repeat these actions to undo previous changes you made.

Tip

How can I enlarge the photo so I can clearly see the area I want to change?

To enlarge a photo for editing, drag the slider ( ) to the right until you can clearly view the area you want to change.

18 To change the photo to black and white, click **B & W**.

■ The photo appears in shades of black and white.

19 To change the photo to sepia, click **Sepia**.

■ The photo appears in shades of brown.

20 When you finish editing the photo, click **Done** to return to your photo library or album.

VIEW A SLIDESHOW OF YOUR PHOTOS

You can view a slideshow of your photos on your computer screen. A slideshow displays one photo at a time.

VIEW A SLIDESHOW OF YOUR PHOTOS

1 Click the album that contains the photos you want to view in a slideshow. You can also click Library to view all your photos.

2 Press and hold down the ⌘ key as you click each photo you want to view in a slideshow.

3 Click **Slideshow**.

■ The first photo that will appear in the slideshow is displayed in this area.

4 Click **Play** to start the full-screen slideshow of the photos you selected.

Tip

Can I rename a slideshow that iPhoto has saved for me?

Yes. To give a slideshow a more meaningful name, double-click the name of the saved slideshow and type the new name. Then press the `return` key.

Tip

How do I delete a slideshow I no longer want to view?

To delete a saved slideshow, click the name of the saved slideshow and then press the `delete` key. In the confirmation dialog box that appears, click **Delete** to delete the slideshow.

■ The slideshow begins and the first photo fills your screen. iPhoto plays background music to accompany the slideshow.

■ iPhoto may zoom in or out of a photo or move a photo across your screen while the photo is displayed.

5 To end the slideshow at any time, click anywhere on your screen.

■ iPhoto saves the slideshow for you so you can play the slideshow again at any time.

■ The name of the saved slideshow appears in this area and displays the ▣ icon.

■ To play a saved slideshow, click the name of the slideshow and then perform steps **4** and **5**.

PRINT PHOTOS

You can produce
a paper copy of
your photos.

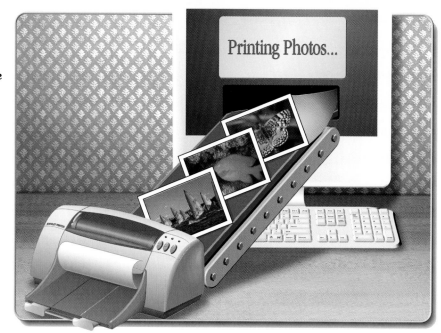

iPhoto offers many
different styles you
can use to print
your photos.

PRINT PHOTOS

1 Click **Library** to
view all your photos
or click the album that
contains the photos
you want to print.

2 Click the photo you
want to print.

■ To print more than
one photo, press and
hold down the ⌘ key as
you click each additional
photo you want to print.

3 Click **Print** to print
the photos you selected.

■ A dialog sheet
appears.

■ This area displays the
printer iPhoto will use.

4 To select a print
setting for your
printer, click this area.

5 Click the setting
you want to use.

Tip

Can I use iPhoto to order professionally printed copies of my photos?

Yes. When your computer is connected to the Internet, you can use iPhoto to order prints of your photos from an online print service.

To order prints of your photos, perform steps **1** and **2** below to select the photos you want to order prints of. Then click **Order Prints**. The Order Prints window appears, displaying an order form you can fill out to order the prints.

*Note: If the **Order Prints** button is not displayed on your screen, click » at the bottom of the iPhoto window to display the option.*

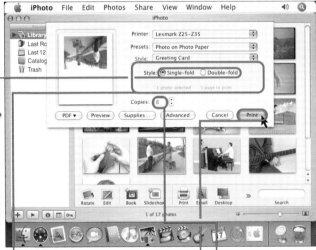

6 To select a print style, click this area.

7 Click the style you want to use.

■ This area shows a preview of how the photos will print.

■ This area displays the options for the style you selected in step **7**. In this example, the Greeting Card options are displayed.

8 Click an option to specify if you want to use the single-fold or double-fold style for your greeting cards (○ changes to ●).

9 To specify the number of copies you want to print, double-click this area and type the number of copies.

10 Click **Print**.

E-MAIL PHOTOS

You can e-mail your photos to a friend, colleague or family member.

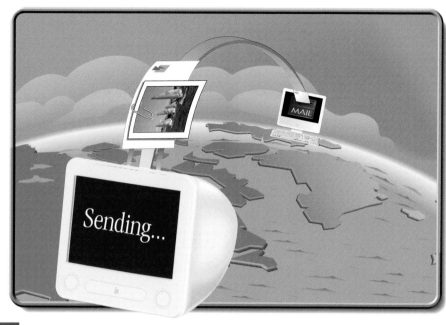

You need to be connected to the Internet to e-mail your photos.

E-MAIL PHOTOS

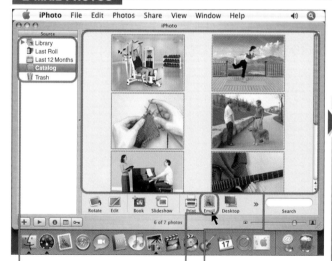

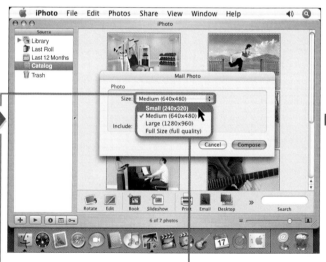

1 Click the album that contains the photos you want to e-mail. You can also click Library to view all your photos.

2 Click the photo you want to e-mail.

Note: To e-mail more than one photo, press and hold down the ⌘ key as you click each photo you want to e-mail.

3 Click **Email** to e-mail the photo(s) you selected.

■ The Mail Photo dialog box appears.

4 To select a size for the photos, click this area.

5 Click the size you want to use for the photos.

Note: Smaller photos transfer faster over the Internet and fit better on the recipient's screen.

Tip

How can I add a title and comments to a photo in my photo library?

You can add a title and comments to a photo to provide a name and description for the photo. The information will be added to every album that contains the photo and will be sent with the photo when you e-mail the photo.

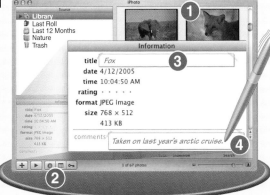

1 Click the photo you want to add a title and comments to.

2 Click ⓘ to display an area where you can add a title and comments.

3 Drag the mouse I over the current title. Then type a new title and press the [return] key.

4 Click this area and type comments for the photo.

■ You can click ⓘ again to hide the title and comments.

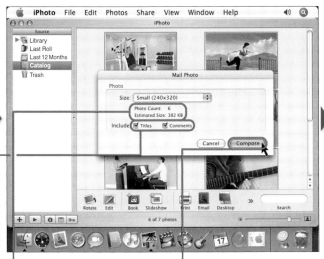

■ This area displays the number of photos you selected and the estimated file size of the photos.

6 These options display the titles and comments for the photos in the e-mail message. You can click an option to display (☑) or hide (☐) the titles or comments.

Note: To add titles and comments to photos, see the top of this page.

7 Click **Compose** to compose the e-mail message.

■ A window appears, allowing you to send the photos in an e-mail message.

8 Click this area and type the e-mail address of the person you want to receive the photos.

9 This area displays a subject for the message. To change the subject, drag the mouse I over the existing subject and then type a new subject.

10 Click this area and type the message you want to accompany the photos.

11 Click **Send** to send the message.

DESIGN A BOOK

After you create an album, you can design a book that beautifully arranges the photos in the album.

Scuba Diving in the Bahamas

The Annual Regatta

iPhoto offers several different book sizes and themes that you can choose for your book.

DESIGN A BOOK

1 Click the album that contains the photos you want to arrange in a book.

Note: To create an album, see page 178.

2 Click **Book** to design a book that arranges the photos in the album.

■ A dialog sheet appears.

3 Click this area to select a hardcover or softcover size for the book you want to create.

4 Click the size of hardcover or softcover book you want to create.

How many photos should be in the album I select to create a book?

You should have enough photos to fill up at least 10 pages of a book that you create. If you create a book that has fewer than 10 pages of photos, blank pages will be printed in the book. The maximum book size is 50 pages.

What book sizes does iPhoto offer?

You can create a small, medium or large book to showcase your photos. A small book measures 3 1/2 by 2 5/8 inches. A medium book measures 8 by 6 inches. A large book measures 11 by 8 1/2 inches.

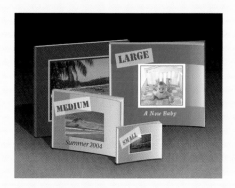

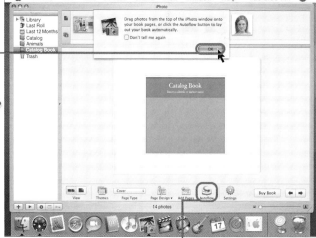

■ This area displays the themes you can choose for your book.

5 Click the theme you want to use for all the pages in the book.

Note: A theme determines the way photos appear on the pages in a book.

■ This area displays a sample of the theme you selected.

6 Click **Choose Theme** to continue.

■ A dialog sheet appears.

7 Click **OK** to continue.

8 Click **Autoflow** to have iPhoto automatically place the photos from your album on the pages in your book.

CONTINUED

DESIGN A BOOK

You can customize the text and photos that appear on each page in a book you design.

When you finish designing a book, you can purchase a printed copy of the book to share with your family and friends.

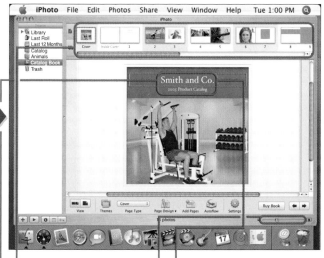

■ This area displays a miniature version of each page in the book.

Note: You can use the scroller to browse through the pages.

■ To view a larger version of a page, click the page.

■ A large version of the current page of the book appears.

9 To edit the text on a page in the book, click the page you want to edit.

10 Click the text you want to edit. A blue box appears around the text.

11 Drag the mouse ‡ over the text you want to edit and type the text you want to appear in the book. Then click outside the blue box.

■ To change the size of the page on your screen, drag this slider (●) to the left or right.

Tip

Why does a ⚠ symbol appear beside a photo in my book?

The ⚠ symbol indicates a photo whose resolution is too low to print properly. A photo displaying the ⚠ symbol may appear jagged or blurry when printed. To improve the resolution of the photo, you can move other photos to the page displaying the photo. More photos on a page will result in the photos printing at a smaller size and a lower resolution.

Tip

How can I change the order of the pages in my book?

To change the order of the pages in a book, position the mouse ▸ over the pages you want to move and then drag the pages to a new location. You cannot move the cover of the book.

12 Repeat steps **9** to **11** for each page that contains text you want to edit.

13 To move a photo to a different page in your book, click the page displaying the photo you want to move.

14 Click the photo you want to move.

15 Drag the photo to the page where you want the photo to appear.

■ A large version of the page appears, displaying the photo you moved to the page. The other photos on the page shift to make room for the new photo.

16 When you have finished making changes to your book, click **Buy Book** to order a printed copy of the book.

■ A window appears, allowing you to order a printed copy of the book. Follow the instructions in the window to purchase a copy of the book.

CHAPTER 8

Create Movies

Read this chapter to find out how to use iMovie to create and work with movies on your computer. You will learn how to transfer video from a digital camcorder, add video clips and transitions to a movie and much more.

TRANSFER VIDEO TO YOUR COMPUTER

You can use iMovie HD to transfer home movies from your camcorder to your computer. You can then edit the video on your computer to create your own movies.

Your screen resolution must be set to 1024 x 768 to work with a movie in iMovie HD. To change your screen resolution, see page 84.

Before you start transferring video from a camcorder, make sure the camcorder is turned on and set to the mode that plays back recorded video. Also make sure the video tape is at the point where you want to begin transferring the video.

TRANSFER VIDEO TO YOUR COMPUTER

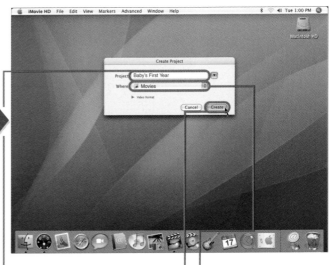

1 Connect your camcorder to your computer.

2 Click the iMovie HD icon to start iMovie HD.

■ A dialog box appears.

3 Click **Create a New Project** to start a new project.

Note: If the dialog box does not appear and you want to transfer video to a new project, see page 202 to create a new project. Then skip to step 6 on page 197.

■ The Create Project dialog box appears.

4 Type a name for the project.

■ This area shows the location where iMovie HD will store the project. You can click this area to change the location.

5 Click **Create** to create the project.

Tip

What is a video clip?

A video clip is a small, manageable segment of a video you transfer to iMovie HD. A video clip is created each time iMovie HD detects a different scene in a video, such as when you turn on your camcorder or when you switch from pause to once again begin recording.

 Tip

How can I delete a video clip?

To delete a video clip you do not plan to use in your movie, click the video clip and then press the `delete` key. The video clip will no longer appear in iMovie HD.

6 Click **Import** to start transferring video to your computer.

■ If Import is not displayed, drag  to the left in this area to display the button.

■ This area displays the video iMovie HD is transferring.

■ As iMovie HD transfers the video, clips for the video appear in the Clips pane. For information on video clips, see the top of this page.

7 When you want to stop transferring the video, click **Import** again.

8 To play a video clip, click the video clip.

9 Click ▶ to play the video clip.

■ The video clip plays in this area.

■ When you finish working with your video, you should save your project. See page 200 to save a project.

10 To quit iMovie HD, click ◯. Then click **Quit** in the dialog box that appears.

197

ADD A VIDEO CLIP TO YOUR MOVIE

You must add each video clip that you want to include in your movie to the clip viewer.

The clip viewer displays the order in which video clips will play in your movie.

You can play a video clip before adding it to your movie to determine if you want to include the video clip in your movie.

ADD A VIDEO CLIP TO YOUR MOVIE

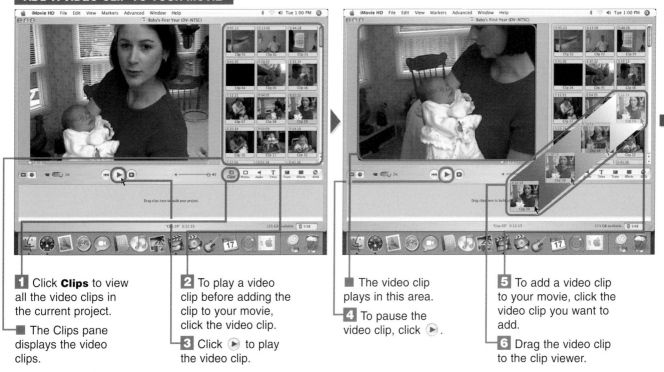

1 Click **Clips** to view all the video clips in the current project.

■ The Clips pane displays the video clips.

2 To play a video clip before adding the clip to your movie, click the video clip.

3 Click ▶ to play the video clip.

■ The video clip plays in this area.

4 To pause the video clip, click ▶.

5 To add a video clip to your movie, click the video clip you want to add.

6 Drag the video clip to the clip viewer.

Tip

Can I change the order of the video clips in the clip viewer?

Yes. Changing the order of the video clips in the clip viewer allows you to change the order in which the clips will play in your movie. To change the location of a video clip in your movie, position the mouse ► over the video clip in the clip viewer and then drag the video clip to a new location in the clip viewer. When you move a video clip, the surrounding video clips will automatically move to make room for the video clip.

■ The video clip appears in the clip viewer.

■ To add other video clips to your movie, repeat steps **5** and **6** for each video clip you want to add.

Note: You can add a video clip before, after or between existing video clips in the clip viewer.

REMOVE A VIDEO CLIP

1 If you no longer want a video clip to appear in your movie, position the mouse ► over the video clip in the clip viewer.

2 Drag the video clip to the Clips pane.

SAVE AND OPEN A PROJECT

You should regularly save changes you make to a project to avoid losing your work. You can also open a saved project to work with the contents of the project.

A project is a rough draft of your movie that contains all the video clips you added to the clip viewer.

SAVE A PROJECT

1 To save the current project, click **File**.

2 Click **Save Project**.

■ iMovie HD saves the changes you made to the project.

OPEN A PROJECT

■ You can work with only one project at a time. Before opening a project, make sure you save your current project.

1 Click **File**.

2 Click **Open Project**.

■ The Open dialog box appears.

Tip

Can iMovie HD automatically open the last project I worked with?

Yes. When you start iMovie HD, the last project you worked with automatically appears on your screen. This allows you to immediately begin working with the project.

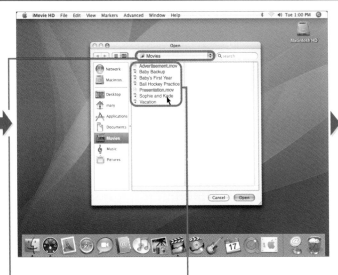

■ This area shows the location of the displayed projects. You can click this area to select a different location.

Note: By default, iMovie HD stores each project you create within your Movies folder. For information on the Movies folder, see page 34.

3 Click the project you want to open.

■ This area displays information about the project you selected.

4 Click **Open** to open the project.

■ The project opens and the video clips in the project appear on your screen.

CREATE A NEW PROJECT

When you want to transfer new video from your camcorder to your computer, you can create a new project to store the video.

A project stores the video clips for a video you transfer from your camcorder and a rough draft of your movie.

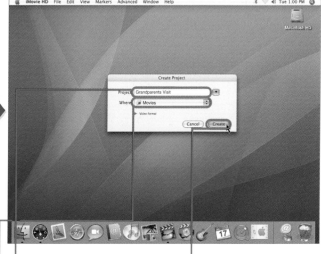

■ You can work with only one project at a time. Before creating a new project, make sure you save your current project. To save a project, see page 200.

1 Click **File**.

2 Click **New Project**.

■ The iMovie HD window closes and the Create Project dialog box appears.

3 Type a name for the project.

■ This area shows the location where iMovie HD will store the project. You can click this area to change the location.

4 Click **Create** to create the project.

■ The iMovie HD window re-opens. You can now perform steps **6** and **7** on page 197 to transfer video from your camcorder into the new project.

CROP A VIDEO CLIP

You can crop the beginning and end of a video clip to remove parts of the clip you do not want to play in your movie.

CROP A VIDEO CLIP

1 Click the video clip you want to crop.

2 To specify where you want the video clip to end, drag the end crop marker (◣) to the location in the video clip.

3 To specify where you want the video clip to start, drag the start crop marker (◢) to the location in the video clip.

■ A yellow area on the bar indicates the part of the video clip that iMovie HD will keep. iMovie HD will remove the parts of the video clip outside of the yellow area.

4 Click **Edit**.

5 Click **Crop** to crop the video clip.

ADD A PHOTO TO A MOVIE

You can add a photo stored in your iPhoto Library to your movie.

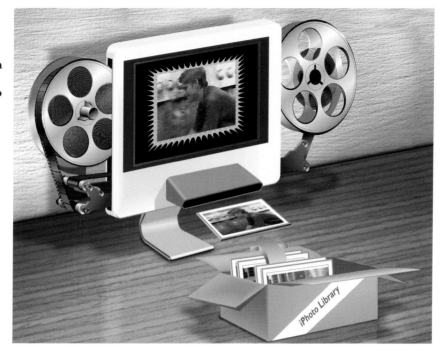

For information on using iPhoto, see pages 176 to 193.

You can use the Ken Burns Effect to zoom in or out of a photo to add motion to a photo in your movie. The Ken Burns Effect is named after Ken Burns, an acclaimed filmmaker.

ADD A PHOTO TO A MOVIE

■1 Click **Photos** to add a photo to your movie.

■ This area displays the photos in your iPhoto Library.

■ To display the photos in an album you created, click this area and then click the name of the album containing the photos you want to use.

■2 Click the photo you want to add to your movie.

■ This area displays the way your photo will appear in the movie.

■ If the photo does not display motion, click the box (☐) beside **Ken Burns Effect** to add motion to the photo (☐ changes to ☑).

■3 To change the starting size of the photo, drag this slider (◯) to the left.

■4 Drag this slider (●) right or left to increase or decrease the starting size of the photo.

Tip

How can I remove the motion from a photo I added to my movie?

You can turn off the Ken Burns Effect to remove motion from a photo in your movie. Displaying still photos is useful if you want to create a slide show in iMovie HD.

1 Click the photo you want to remove motion from in the clip viewer.

2 Click **Photos** to display the photo options.

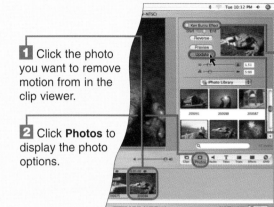

3 Click the box (☑) beside **Ken Burns Effect** (☑ changes to ☐).

4 Click **Update** to update the photo in your movie.

5 To change the finished size of the photo, perform steps **3** and **4**, except drag the slider (◯) to the right in step **3**.

6 To change the duration of the motion, drag this slider (◯) left or right.

7 To preview your changes, click **Preview**.

8 To add the photo to your movie, click **Apply**.

■ The photo appears after the last video clip in the clip viewer. To move the photo to a new location in the movie, see the top of page 199.

■ To delete a photo from your movie, click the photo and then press the delete key.

ADD A VIDEO TRANSITION

You can add an interesting video transition from one video clip to another in your movie. Adding video transitions between video clips blends the end of one video clip with the beginning of the next video clip.

ADD A VIDEO TRANSITION

1 Click **Trans** to add a video transition to your movie.

■ This area displays the video transitions you can add to your movie.

2 To see a preview of how a video transition will appear in your movie, click the transition.

■ This area displays a preview of the video transition.

■ If you selected the **Billow** or **Push** transitions in step **2**, click an arrow in this area to specify the direction you want the video clip to move off the screen.

3 To decrease or increase the length of time that the transition occurs in your movie, drag this slider (⬤) left or right.

Tip

How do I remove a video transition from my movie?

To remove a video transition, click the picture representing the transition between the video clips in the clip viewer. Then press the delete key.

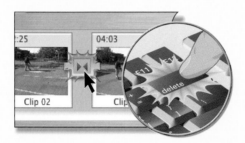

Tip

What should I consider when adding video transitions to a movie?

Although iMovie HD offers many different types of video transitions, using too many different transitions in a movie can distract the audience from your movie. If you are trying to create a professional-looking movie, use similar video transitions throughout your movie and add video transitions sparingly.

4 To add a video transition to your movie, position the mouse ▸ over the transition you want to add.

5 Drag the video transition between the video clips on the clip viewer where you want to add the transition.

■ A small picture representing the video transition appears between the video clips.

■ To add additional video transitions to your movie, repeat steps **2** to **5** for each transition you want to add.

6 To play the transition between the video clips, click the picture representing the transition.

7 Click ▸ to play the transition in your movie.

■ The transition plays in this area.

PREVIEW A MOVIE

After you add the video clips you want to include in your movie, you can preview how the movie will play.

PREVIEW A MOVIE

1 To preview a movie, click (⏮) to move to the beginning of the movie.

■ To preview only one video clip in the movie, click the video clip. The video clip is highlighted.

2 Click (▶) to preview the movie.

■ The movie plays in this area.

■ You can click (▶) again to stop playing the movie.

■ This slider (▽) indicates the progress of the movie. The amount of time the movie has been playing appears next to the slider.

Tip

When should I preview a movie I have created?

You should preview a movie you have created before you save the completed movie to make sure you are happy with the movie. You can also preview a movie at any time while you create the movie.

Tip

Can I preview a movie using the entire screen?

Yes. You can click ⊙ to preview a movie using the entire screen. To return to iMovie HD, click anywhere on your screen.

■ Vertical lines on the bar indicate where each video clip begins and ends in the movie.

■ The slider (▽) moves to the new location.

3 To quickly move to a specific location in your movie, click the location on the bar.

■ A red marker (|) in the video clips also indicates the progress of the movie.

4 To decrease or increase the volume of the movie, drag this slider (●) left or right.

SAVE A MOVIE AS A QUICKTIME MOVIE

After you finish creating a movie, you can save the movie as a QuickTime movie on your computer.

Saving a movie as a QuickTime movie on your computer allows you to share the movie with family and friends.

SAVE A MOVIE AS A QUICKTIME MOVIE

1 To save the video clips in the clip viewer as a QuickTime movie, click **File**.

2 Click **Share**.

■ A dialog sheet appears.

3 Click **QuickTime** to save your movie as a QuickTime movie.

4 To specify the format you want to use for your movie, click this area to display a list of the available formats.

5 Click the format you want to use.

Note: For information on the available formats, see the top of page 211.

Tip

Which format should I select for my movie?

The format you should select depends on how you intend to use the movie.

Format:	Intended Use:
Email	Send the movie in an e-mail message.
Web	Publish the movie to the Web.
Web Streaming	Publish the movie to a QuickTime streaming Web server, which plays movies on the Web as they are downloading.
CD-ROM	Copy the movie to a recordable CD.
Full Quality	Work with the movie in another application.

Tip

How can I later play a movie I have saved as a QuickTime movie?

iMovie HD automatically stores your movies in the Movies folder, which is located within your Home folder. You can double-click a movie in the Movies folder to open the movie in a QuickTime Player window. For information on playing movies using QuickTime Player, see page 170.

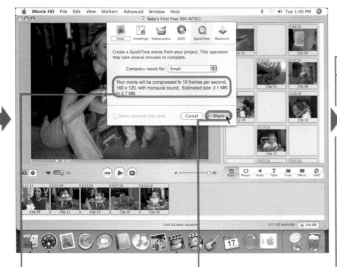

■ This area displays information about how the movie will be compressed and saved.

6 Click **Share** to save the movie.

■ The Save dialog box appears.

7 Type a name for the movie.

■ This area shows the location where iMovie HD will store the movie. You can click this area to change the location.

8 Click **Save** to save the movie.

■ A progress dialog sheet remains on your screen until iMovie HD has finished saving your movie.

USER ACCOUNTS
TOM
SALLY
JENN
West Parkdale Auto Shop
Location
Hours of Operation

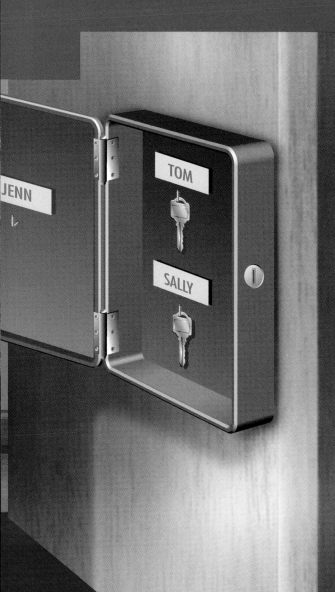

Share Your Computer

If you share your computer with other people, you can create a separate user account for each person. In this chapter, you will learn how to create and manage user accounts on your computer.

ADD A USER ACCOUNT

If you share your computer with other people, you can create a separate user account for each person.

You must have an administrator account to add a user account to your computer.

ADD A USER ACCOUNT

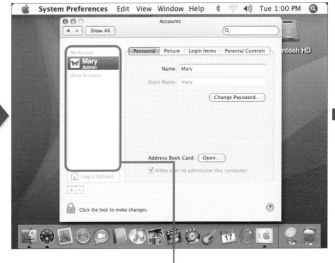

1 Click the System Preferences icon to access your system preferences.

■ The System Preferences window appears.

2 Click **Accounts** to work with the user accounts on your computer.

■ The Accounts window appears.

■ This area lists the names of the user accounts that are currently on your computer.

Note: When Mac OS X was installed on your computer, an administrator account was created.

Will Mac OS X keep my personal files separate from the files of other users?

Yes. Mac OS X will keep your personal files separate from the personal files created by other users. For example, your home folder contains only the files you have created. Safari also keeps your lists of recently visited Web pages and bookmarks separate from the lists of other users.

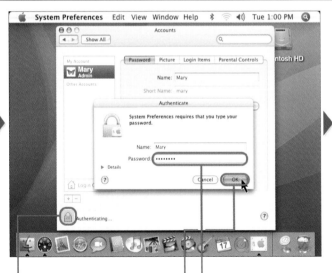

How can I personalize Mac OS X for my user account?

You can personalize the appearance of Mac OS X for your user account by changing the screen saver, desktop picture and many other computer settings.

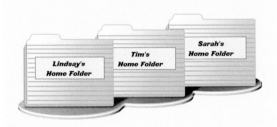

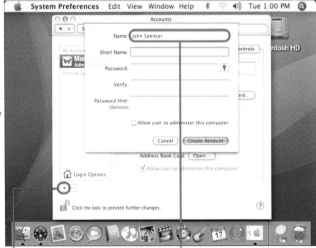

3 To be able to work with user accounts on your computer, click the lock (🔒).

*Note: If the lock is open (🔓), skip to step **6**.*

■ A dialog box appears, displaying your user name.

4 Type the password for your user account.

5 Click **OK** to change the user account settings on your computer.

6 Click + to add a new user account to your computer.

■ A dialog sheet appears, allowing you to enter information about the new user.

7 Click this area and type the full name of the person who will use the new user account. Then press the **tab** key.

CONTINUED ▶

ADD A USER ACCOUNT

When you add a user account, you must create a password for the account. A password helps prevent other people from accessing the account. The user will need to enter the password each time they want to use Mac OS X.

You should choose a password that contains a random combination of letters, numbers and symbols. Do not use words that people can easily associate with you, such as your name.

ADD A USER ACCOUNT (CONTINUED)

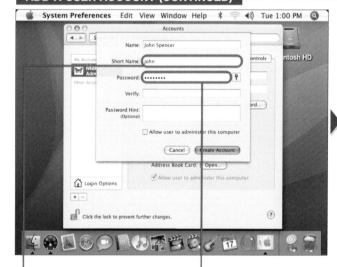

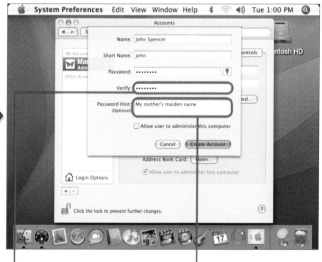

8 This area displays a short name for the person. To change the short name, drag the mouse I over the name until the name is highlighted and then type a new short name.

Note: A short name cannot contain spaces.

9 Click this area and type a password for the user account.

Note: A password will prevent unauthorized people from accessing the user account.

10 Click this area and type the password again to confirm the password.

11 To include a password hint that will help the person remember the password, click this area and type the password hint.

Tip

Can I edit the information for a user account?

If you have an administrator account, you can make changes to any user account on the computer. To edit the information for a user account, perform the steps starting on page 214, selecting the name of the user account you want to edit in step **6**. To change the password for a user account, click **Reset Password** to display a dialog sheet where you can type and confirm the new password.

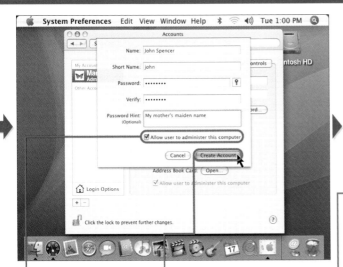

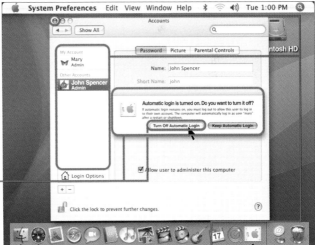

12 To set the account as an administrator account and allow the person to perform administrative tasks on the computer, click this option (☐ changes to ☑).

Note: An administrator can perform any task on the computer, such as installing new programs. A standard user can perform only limited tasks on the computer, such as personalizing some settings.

13 Click **Create Account** to create the user account.

■ The first time you add a new user account, a dialog box appears, stating that the automatic login feature is turned on. For more information on automatic login, see page 222.

*Note: If the dialog box does not appear, skip to step **15**.*

14 To turn off the automatic login feature and require a user to log in when the computer starts, click **Turn Off Automatic Login**.

■ The new user account appears in this area.

15 To close the Accounts window, click ◉ .

DELETE A USER ACCOUNT

If a person no longer uses your computer, you can delete the person's user account from the computer.

You must have an administrator account to delete a user account.

DELETE A USER ACCOUNT

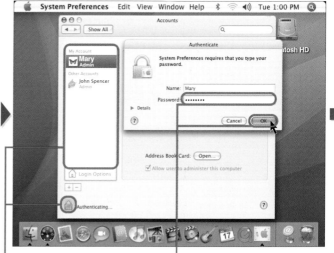

1 Click the System Preferences icon to access your system preferences.

■ The System Preferences window appears.

2 Click **Accounts** to work with the user accounts on your computer.

■ The Accounts window appears.

■ This area lists the names of the user accounts on your computer.

3 To be able to work with user accounts on your computer, click the lock (🔒).

Note: If the lock is open (🔓), skip to step 6.

■ A dialog box appears, displaying your user name.

4 Type the password for your user account.

5 Click **OK** to change the user account settings on your computer.

Tip

If I choose to keep the contents of the home folder for a deleted user account, how can I later access the contents of the folder?

If you choose to save the contents of the home folder for a deleted user account, the contents will be saved in the Deleted Users folder. To open the folder, double-click the hard disk icon on your desktop. In the window that appears, double-click the **Users** folder and then double-click the **Deleted Users** folder.

In the Deleted Users folder, double-click the icon for the deleted user account to open a window displaying the user's folders. Mac OS X also places a disk icon for the deleted user account on your desktop. You can double-click the disk icon to access the contents of the home folder for the user account at any time.

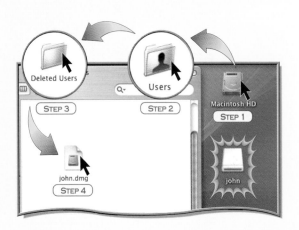

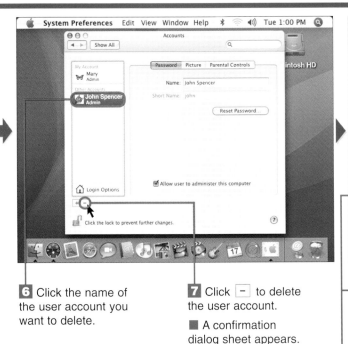

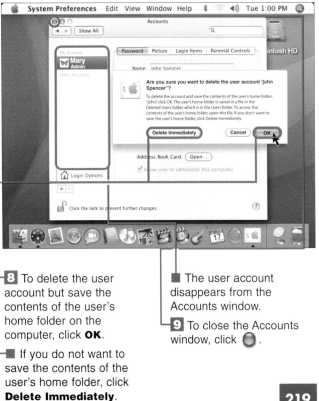

6 Click the name of the user account you want to delete.

7 Click – to delete the user account.

■ A confirmation dialog sheet appears.

8 To delete the user account but save the contents of the user's home folder on the computer, click **OK**.

■ If you do not want to save the contents of the user's home folder, click **Delete Immediately**.

■ The user account disappears from the Accounts window.

9 To close the Accounts window, click .

LOG OUT OR LOG IN

When you finish using your computer, you can log out so another person can log in to use the computer.

Logging out leaves the computer on, but exits your user account. Logging in allows you to specify the user account you want to use.

LOG OUT

■ Before you log out, make sure you close any applications you have open.

1 Click to display the Apple menu.

2 Click **Log Out** to log out.

Note: The name of the Log Out command depends on the name of the current user.

■ A dialog box appears, confirming that you want to log out.

3 Click **Log Out** to log out.

*Note: If you do not perform step **3** within 2 minutes, your computer will log you out automatically.*

■ The login window appears, allowing another person to log in to use the computer.

Why does my login window look different than the login window shown below?

Your login window will look different if you chose to have each user enter both their account name and password to log in. For information on changing the login options, see page 222.

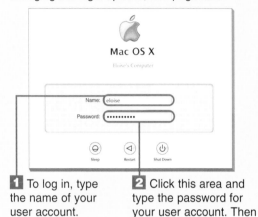

1 To log in, type the name of your user account.

2 Click this area and type the password for your user account. Then press the return key.

 Why did the login window shake when I tried to log in?

The login window shakes when you enter an incorrect password. If you enter an incorrect password three times, your password hint may appear. After reading the password hint, try entering your password again.

LOG IN

■ When you log out, the login window appears.

Note: The login window also appears each time you turn on your computer if the automatic login option is turned off. To turn off the automatic login option, see page 222.

■ This area displays the names of the user accounts on your computer.

1 Click the name of your user account.

■ If you assigned a password to your user account, a box appears that allows you to enter your password.

2 Type your password and then press the return key to log in.

■ If you accidentally selected the wrong name, you can click **Go Back** to select another name.

■ Mac OS X starts, displaying your personalized settings.

221

CHANGE THE WAY USERS LOG IN

You can change the login options to customize the way you and other users log in to Mac OS X.

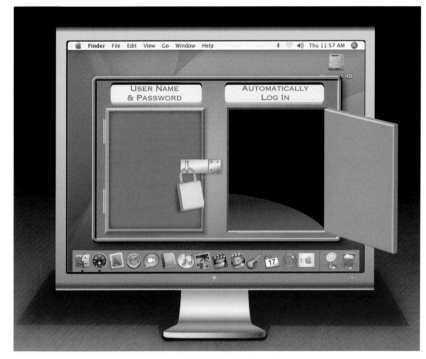

You must have an administrator account to change the way users log in.

CHANGE THE WAY USERS LOG IN

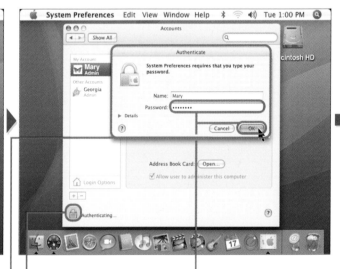

1 Click the System Preferences icon to access your system preferences.

■ The System Preferences window appears.

2 Click **Accounts** to work with the user accounts on your computer.

■ The Accounts window appears.

3 To be able to change the way users log in, click the lock (🔒).

Note: If the lock is open (🔓), skip to step 6.

■ A dialog box appears, displaying your user name.

4 Type the password for your user account.

5 Click **OK** to change the way users log in.

Tip

If the computer uses my account to automatically log in, how can other users log in using their accounts?

When you finish using the computer, you can log out so another user can log in using their account. Logging out exits your user account, but leaves the computer on and ready for another user to log in. For information on logging in or out, see page 220. You can also switch between users without logging out. For information on switching between users, see page 226.

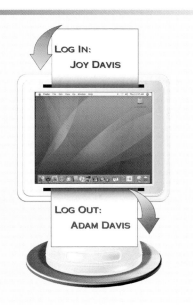

LOG IN:
JOY DAVIS

LOG OUT:
ADAM DAVIS

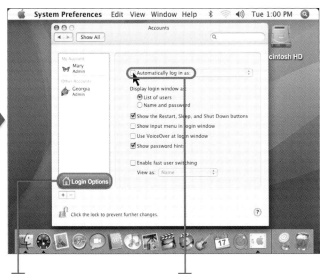

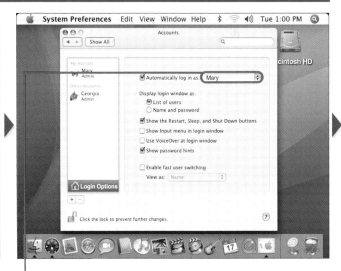

6 Click **Login Options** to display the login options that you can change.

7 You can click this option to turn the automatic login feature on (☑) or off (☐).

■ When automatic login is turned on, the user account displayed in this area will be automatically logged in every time the computer starts.

Note: When automatic login is turned off, each user must specify their account name and password to log in before using the computer.

CONTINUED

CHANGE THE WAY USERS LOG IN

If you have more than one user account on your computer, you can specify which account you want to use to automatically log in to Mac OS X each time you turn on the computer.

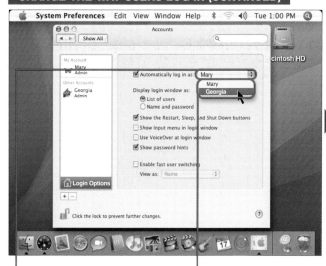

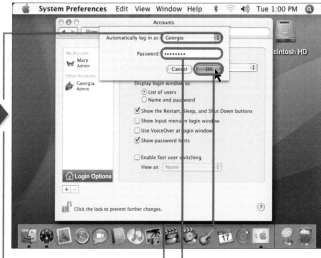

8 To change the user account you want to be automatically logged in every time the computer starts, click this area.

9 Click the user account you want to be automatically logged in.

■ A dialog sheet appears.

■ This area displays the name of the user account you selected.

10 Type the password for the user account.

11 Click **OK** to confirm the information you entered.

Tip

What other changes can I make to the login window?

Mac OS X provides several options you can select to change the appearance of the login window. For example, you can disable the Restart, Sleep and Shut Down buttons in the login window to help prevent unauthorized access to your computer. You can also turn on the Use VoiceOver at login window option to have VoiceOver read the contents of the login window to you. For more information on VoiceOver, see page 110.

After performing steps 1 to 6 starting on page 222, you can click a login option in the Accounts window to turn the option on (✓) or off (▢).

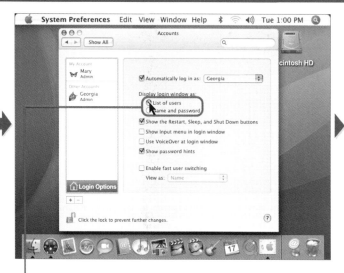

12 You can click an option to specify how you want users to specify their user account in the login window (◯ changes to ◉).

List of users
Display a list of user account names in the login window.

Name and password
Display areas where a user can enter the user name and password to login.

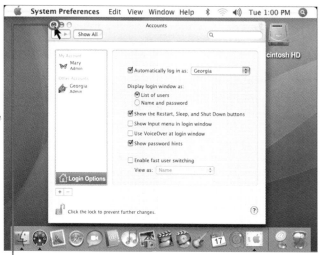

13 To close the Accounts window and save your changes, click ◯.

QUICKLY SWITCH BETWEEN USERS

Mac OS X allows you to quickly switch between users on the computer. This allows you to keep your applications and files open while another person uses the computer.

Switching between users allows you to quickly return to your applications and files after another person finishes using the computer.

TURN ON FAST USER SWITCHING

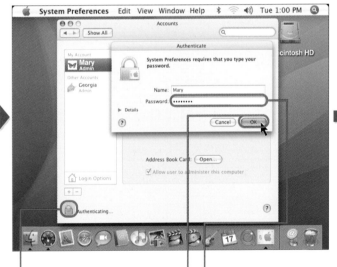

■ Before you can quickly switch between users, you must turn on the fast user switching feature.

1 Click the System Preferences icon to access your system preferences.

■ The System Preferences window appears.

2 Click **Accounts** to access the fast user switching feature.

■ The Accounts window appears.

3 To be able to change the user account settings on your computer, click the lock (🔒).

Note: If the lock is open (🔓), skip to step 6.

■ A dialog box appears, displaying your user name.

4 Type the password for your user account.

5 Click **OK** to change the user account settings on your computer.

Tip

After I turn on fast user switching, how do I quickly switch between users on my computer?

1 Click the user name or 👤 icon displayed at the top of your screen. A list of user accounts appears.

2 Click the name of the user account you want to switch to.

■ If you assigned a password to the user account, the login window appears, displaying an area where you can enter the password.

Note: For more information on the login window, see page 221.

3 Type the password and then press the return key to log in.

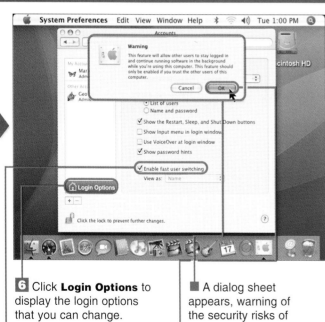

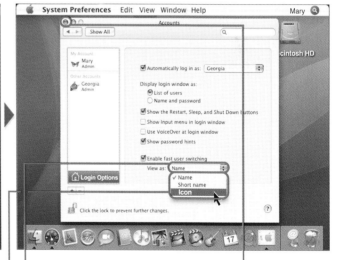

6 Click **Login Options** to display the login options that you can change.

7 Click this option to allow quickly switching between users without quitting your applications (🔲 changes to ☑).

■ A dialog sheet appears, warning of the security risks of fast user switching.

8 Click **OK** to continue.

9 Click this area to choose how you want user names to appear in the menu bar for fast user switching.

10 Click the way you want user names to appear in the menu bar.

Name—Displays the full user name of the current user account.

Short name—Displays the short name for the current user account.

Icon—Displays the 👤 icon.

11 To close the Accounts window, click 🔴.

■ You can now quickly switch between users at any time.

SET PARENTAL CONTROLS

Parental controls allow you to keep children safe and prevent them from viewing inappropriate information while they use the computer. You can set parental controls for Safari to specify which Web sites a user can access.

When you set parental controls for Safari, a user can access only the Web sites that have been added to the Bookmarks Bar for the user.

SET PARENTAL CONTROLS

1 Click the System Preferences icon to access your system preferences.

■ The System Preferences window appears.

2 Click **Accounts** to work with the user accounts on your computer.

■ The Accounts window appears.

3 To be able to work with user accounts on your computer, click the lock (🔒).

Note: If the lock is open (🔓), skip to step 5.

■ A dialog box appears, displaying your user name.

4 Type the password for your user account and then press the return key to change the user account settings on your computer.

What must I do after turning on parental controls for Safari in the Accounts window?

After turning on parental controls for Safari in the Accounts window, you must log in to Mac OS X as the user you set up parental controls for. To log in as a different user, see page 220. You can then open Safari and create a bookmark for each Web site you want the user to be able to access. The bookmarks you create must be stored in the Bookmarks Bar. To create bookmarks, see page 264.

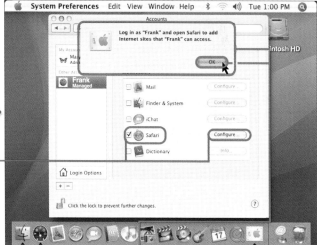

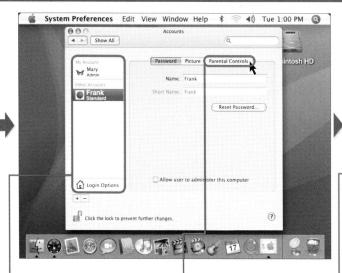

■ This area lists the names of the user accounts that are currently on your computer.

5 Click the user account you want to set parental controls for.

Note: You can only set parental controls for standard user accounts.

6 Click **Parental Controls** to set parental controls for the user account.

PARENTAL CONTROLS FOR SAFARI

7 To set parental controls for Safari, click **Safari** (changes to ✓).

8 Click **Configure**.

■ A dialog sheet appears, asking you to log in as the user you are setting parental controls for and open Safari to add Web sites that the user can access. For more information, see the top of this page.

9 Click **OK** to close the dialog sheet.

CONTINUED

SET PARENTAL CONTROLS

You can set parental controls for Mail to specify which e-mail addresses a user can exchange e-mail messages with.

When you set parental controls for Mail, you can specify that any messages from unapproved e-mail addresses should be sent to another e-mail address, such as your own, for approval.

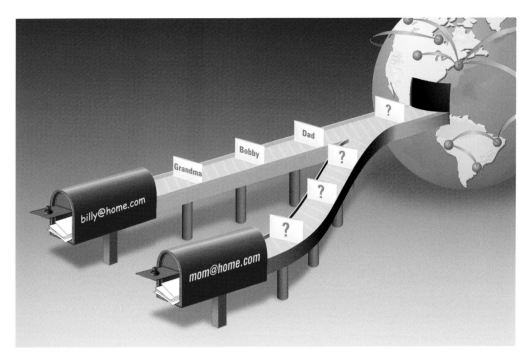

SET PARENTAL CONTROLS (CONTINUED)

PARENTAL CONTROLS FOR MAIL

10 Click **Mail** to set parental controls for Mail (☐ changes to ☑).

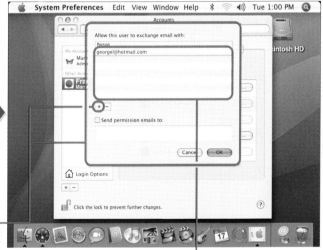

■ A dialog sheet appears.

11 To add the e-mail address of a person the user is allowed to exchange e-mail messages with, click ⊞ .

12 Type the e-mail address and then press the `return` key.

Tip

Can I later add other acceptable e-mail addresses to the parental controls?

Yes. In the Accounts window, click the **Configure** button beside Mail to display the dialog sheet that allows you to enter acceptable e-mail addresses. Perform steps **11** and **12** below to enter each acceptable e-mail address and then click **OK** to close the dialog sheet.

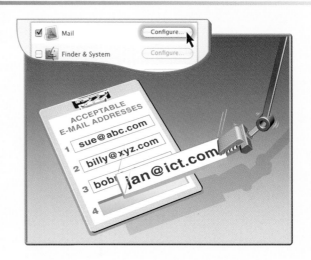

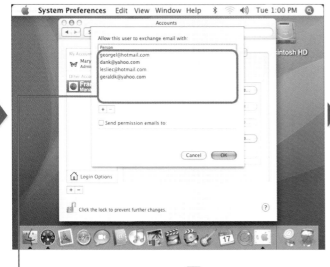

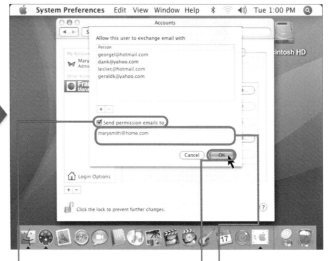

■ The e-mail address you typed appears in this area.

13 Repeat steps **11** and **12** for each e-mail address you want the user to be allowed to exchange e-mail messages with.

14 When e-mail messages arrive from addresses that are not in the list you specified, you can have the messages sent to another e-mail address for approval before the user sees the e-mail messages. Click this option (☐ changes to ☑).

15 Type the e-mail address you want to send unapproved e-mail messages to for approval.

16 Click **OK** to close the dialog sheet.

CONTINUED ▶

SET PARENTAL CONTROLS

You can set parental controls for iChat to specify the people that a user can exchange instant messages with.

After you set parental controls for iChat, people that you have not approved will not be able to see the user's online status or contact the user.

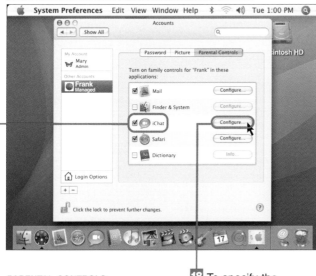

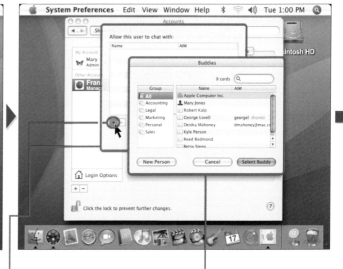

PARENTAL CONTROLS FOR iCHAT

17 Click **iChat** to set parental controls for iChat (☐ changes to ☑).

18 To specify the people the user will be able to chat with, click **Configure**.

■ A dialog sheet appears.

19 To add a person the user is allowed to exchange instant messages with, click ➕.

■ The Buddies window appears, displaying a list of the people in Address Book.

Note: For information on Address Book, see page 124.

Tip

Are there other parental controls I can set in Mac OS X?

You can set parental controls for Mac OS X to specify which applications and features on the computer a user can access and work with. Choose **Finder & System** in the Accounts window (☐ changes to ☑) and then click the **Configure** button beside Finder & System to set up the parental controls for Mac OS X applications and features.

You can also set parental controls for the Dictionary to prevent a user from being able to access certain terms, such as profanity, in the Dictionary. Choose **Dictionary** in the Accounts window (☐ changes to ☑).

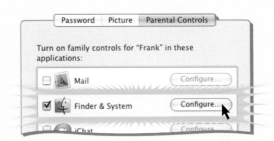

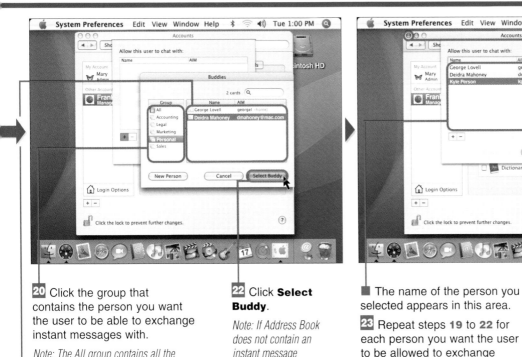

20 Click the group that contains the person you want the user to be able to exchange instant messages with.

Note: The All group contains all the people in Address Book.

21 Click the person you want the user to be able to exchange instant messages with.

22 Click **Select Buddy**.

Note: If Address Book does not contain an instant message account for the person, see the top of page 297 to enter the required information.

■ The name of the person you selected appears in this area.

23 Repeat steps **19** to **22** for each person you want the user to be allowed to exchange instant messages with.

24 Click **OK** to close the dialog sheet.

25 To close the Accounts window, click ●.

VIEW SHARED FILES

You can view the files shared by every user on your computer.

VIEW SHARED FILES

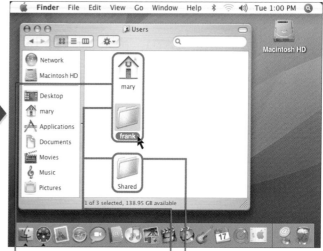

1 Double-click your hard disk icon on the desktop to view the contents of your hard disk.

■ A window appears, displaying the contents of your hard disk.

2 Double-click **Users** to display the contents of the Users folder.

■ The Users window appears, displaying the home folder for each user account on your computer. The home folder for your user account displays a house icon (🏠).

■ The Shared folder contains files shared by the users on your computer. Every user can use this folder to share files.

3 To display the contents of a folder, double-click the folder.

Tip

How can I share my files with other users?

Shared Folder	Public Folder	Drop Box
To share files with every user on your computer, press and hold down the option key as you drag the files to the Shared folder within the Users folder. Every user can view and add files in this folder, but cannot make changes to the files. Only a user with an administrator account can delete files that other users have added to this folder.	To share files with every user on your computer, press and hold down the option key as you drag the files to the Public folder within the home folder for your user account. Every user can view the files in this folder, but cannot make changes to the files or add files to the folder. Only a user with an administrator account can delete files that you have placed in your Public folder.	To share files with a specific user, press and hold down the option key as you drag the files to the Drop Box folder within the home folder for the user's account. Only the user who owns the Drop Box folder can open the folder to view, change or delete the files.

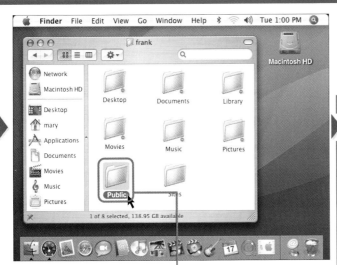

■ In this example, the personal folders for the **frank** user account appear.

Note: If you are viewing the personal folders for a user account other than your own, you can access only the contents of the Public and Sites folders. You cannot access folders that display the ⊖ symbol.

■ The Public folder contains files shared by the owner of the current user account.

4 To display the contents of the Public folder, double-click the folder.

■ The contents of the Public folder appear.

■ The Drop Box folder contains files other users have shared with the owner of the current user account. Only the owner of the Drop Box folder can open this folder.

■ You can click ◀ or ▶ to move backward or forward through the folders you have viewed.

5 When you finish browsing through the shared files on your computer, click ⊖ to close the window.

CHAPTER 10

Work on a Network

A network is a group of connected computers. This chapter teaches you how to share files and printers on a network and how to connect to a wireless network.

TURN ON FILE AND PRINTER SHARING

If you want to share your files and printer with other people on your network, you must turn on file and printer sharing.

Sharing files is useful when other people on your network need to access your files. Sharing a printer allows you to reduce costs since several people on a network can use the same printer.

TURN ON FILE AND PRINTER SHARING

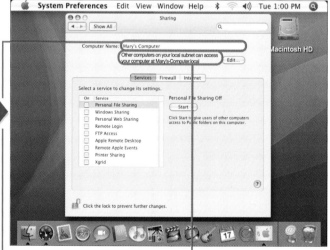

1 Click the System Preferences icon to access your system preferences.

■ The System Preferences window appears.

2 Click **Sharing** to share your files and a printer connected to your computer.

■ The Sharing window appears.

■ This area displays your computer name. To change the name, drag the mouse ⊥ over the current name until the name is highlighted. Then type a new name.

■ This area displays the name used to identify your computer to Bonjour-compatible services and applications, such as iChat.

Tip

How can I print files using a shared printer on my network?

You can print files to a shared printer on your network as if the printer was directly connected to your computer. When you print a file, the shared printer will automatically appear in the list of available printers. To print a file, see page 64.

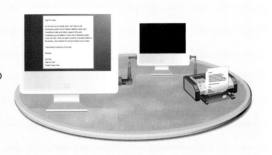

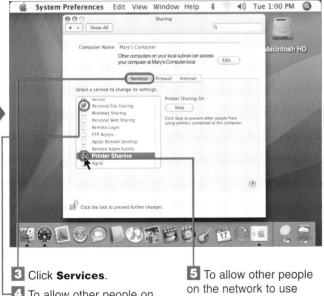

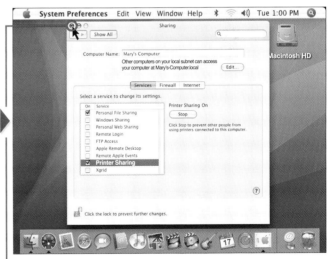

3 Click **Services**.

4 To allow other people on the network to access files you share on your computer, click the box (☐) beside **Personal File Sharing** (☐ changes to ☑).

5 To allow other people on the network to use a printer connected to your computer, click the box (☐) beside **Printer Sharing** (☐ changes to ☑).

■ Everyone on the network can now access files in the Public folder on your computer and use your printer to print documents.

Note: To add files you want to share to your Public folder, see page 240.

6 To close the Sharing window, click ⬤ .

■ To turn off file and printer sharing, perform steps **1** to **6** (☑ changes to ☐ in steps **4** and **5**).

SHARE FILES ON A NETWORK

You can share files with other people on your network by adding the files to the Public folder on your computer. Everyone on the network can access files stored in your Public folder.

Everyone on the network can open and copy, but not change or delete files in your Public folder.

SHARE FILES ON A NETWORK

■ To allow other people on your network to access files you share on your computer, you must turn on file sharing. To turn on file sharing, see page 238.

To turn on file sharing, see page 238.

■1 Click **Go**.

Note: If Go is not available, click a blank area on your desktop to display the Finder menu bar.

■2 Click **Home** to view your personal folders.

■ A window appears, displaying your personal folders.

■3 Double-click the **Public** folder to display the contents of the folder.

Tip

What is the purpose of the Drop Box folder in my Public folder?

The Drop Box folder provides a location where other people on the network can place files they want to share with you. You are the only person who can open your Drop Box folder to view and work with its contents.

Tip

How can I stop sharing a file?

To stop sharing a file, you must remove the file from your Public folder. To display the contents of your Public folder, perform steps **1** to **3** below. Position the mouse ⬉ over the file you no longer want to share and then drag the file out of the Public window.

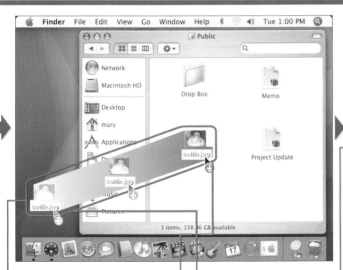

■ The Public window appears, displaying the contents of your Public folder.

4 Locate the file on your computer that you want to share with other people on your network.

5 Position the mouse ⬉ over the file.

6 Press and hold down the option key as you drag the file to the Public window (⬉ changes to ⊕).

■ A copy of the file appears in the Public window.

■ You can repeat steps **4** to **6** for each file you want to share.

Note: You can copy folders to your Public folder the same way you copy files.

7 When you finish copying the files you want to share to your Public folder, click ⬤ to close the Public window.

ACCESS SHARED FILES ON A NETWORK

You can view the files shared by other people on your network.

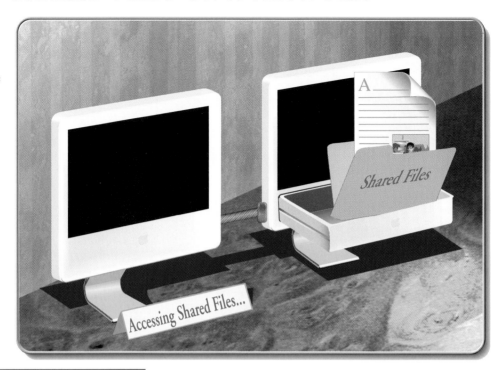

ACCESS SHARED FILES ON A NETWORK

1 Click **Go**.

Note: If Go is not available, click a blank area on your desktop to display the Finder menu bar.

2 Click **Network**.

■ The Network window appears.

3 Click the network or workgroup containing the computer you want to access.

■ This area displays the computers on the network or workgroup that have file or printer sharing turned on. For information on file or printer sharing, see page 238.

4 Click the computer that contains the shared files you want to access.

5 Click **Connect** to see the available files on the computer you selected.

What files can I access on my network?

You can access files that other users on your network have added to their Public folders. To access the shared files in a user's Public folder, the computer that stores the files must be turned on and have file sharing turned on. For information on adding files to the Public folder, see page 240. For information on turning on file sharing, see page 238.

Can I quickly access the computers on my network while I'm working in a Finder window?

You can click **Network** in the Sidebar of any open Finder window on your computer to quickly display the Network window. You can then perform steps **3** to **15** starting on page 242 to access the computers and shared files on the network. For more information on using the Sidebar, see page 20.

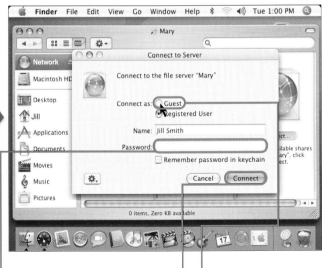

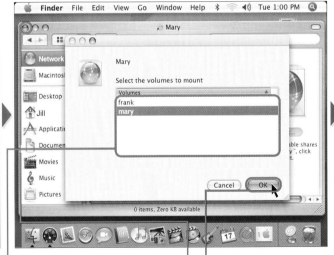

■ The Connect to Server dialog box appears.

■ To connect to the computer as a registered user, type your password and then press the return key.

Note: Registered users may have fewer restrictions than users who connect as guests.

6 To connect to the computer as a guest, click **Guest** (○ changes to ●).

7 Click **Connect**.

■ A dialog box appears, displaying the names of the user accounts that you can access on the computer.

8 Click the name of the user account that shared the files you want to access.

9 Click **OK** to continue.

10 To close the Network window, click ●.

CONTINUED ▶

When viewing shared files on a computer on your network, you can open the files, but you cannot change or delete the files.

ACCESS SHARED FILES ON A NETWORK (CONTINUED)

■ An icon for the user account you selected appears on your desktop.

11 Double-click the icon to access the files shared by the user.

■ A window appears, displaying the files shared by the user.

■ To open a file, double-click the file.

ADD FILES TO THE DROP BOX FOLDER

■ The Drop Box folder provides a location where you can place files you want to share with the owner of the user account.

Note: Only the owner of the user account can view and work with the contents of the Drop Box.

Tip

How can I make changes to a shared file on my network?

You cannot make changes to a shared file on the network, but you can create a copy of the file on your computer and then work with the copy on your computer. To make a copy of a shared file, position the mouse ▶ over the file you want to copy and then drag the file to your desktop.

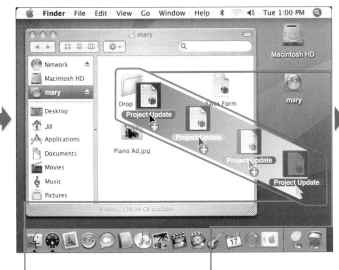

12 To share a file on your computer with the owner of the user account, position the mouse ▶ over the file.

13 Drag the file to the Drop Box folder (▶ changes to ⬆).

■ A dialog box appears, stating that you do not have permission to see the results of the copy.

14 Click **OK** to copy the file to the Drop Box folder.

15 When you finish working with the shared files, you can click ⬤ to close the window.

CONNECT TO A WIRELESS NETWORK

You can connect to a wireless network to access the information and equipment available on the network without using cables or phone lines.

If a wireless network is connected to the Internet, connecting to the network will also allow you to access the Internet.

Your computer must have AirPort or wireless networking capabilities to connect to a wireless network. The network must also have wireless networking capabilities, such as an AirPort Base Station, and be within range of your computer.

Connecting to a wireless network...

CONNECT TO A WIRELESS NETWORK

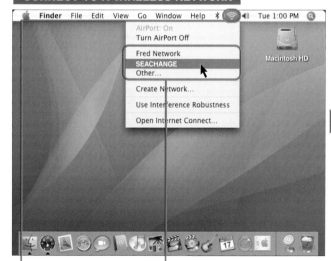

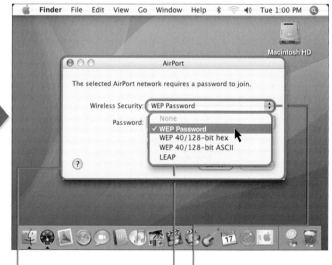

1 Click 🛜 to connect to a wireless network.

■ A menu appears.

■ This area lists all the wireless networks that are available to you.

2 Click the wireless network you want to connect to.

■ If the network requires you to enter a password to gain access to the network, the AirPort dialog box appears.

Note: A password helps protect a network by preventing unauthorized people from accessing the network.

3 Click this area to display a list of password types you can choose from for the network.

4 Click the type of password you need to enter to gain access to the network.

Can I connect to a wireless network when I am away from home or the office?

Increasing numbers of public places, such as coffee shops, hotels and airports, are allowing people to connect to the Internet through wireless networks set up on their premises. These locations are called wi-fi hotspots, or wireless hotspots, and provide a convenient way of accessing the Internet while you are away from home or the office.

 How can I ensure a good connection to a wireless network?

When connecting to a wireless network, the strength of the radio signal used to connect to the network is very important. For the best signal, try to avoid obstacles between your computer and the wireless network. Also try to avoid using devices that use the same frequency as your wireless network, such as a cordless phone, near the network.

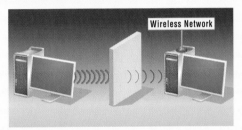

5 Type the password required to gain access to the network.

*Note: Some wireless networks require you to type **0x** in front of the password in order to gain access to the network.*

6 Click **OK**.

■ The AirPort icon in the Finder menu bar indicates if you are connected (icon) or not connected (icon) to a wireless network.

Note: You only need to perform steps 1 to 6 once to connect to a wireless network. The next time you are within range of the last wireless network you were connected to, Mac OS X will automatically connect you to the network.

CHAPTER 11

Browse the Web

This chapter explains how to view and work with Web pages. Learn how to display a specific Web page or a list of Web pages you have previously viewed, block unwanted pop-up windows, change your home page and more.

INTRODUCTION TO THE WEB

The Web consists of a huge collection of electronic documents stored on computers around the world. The Web is also known as the World Wide Web.

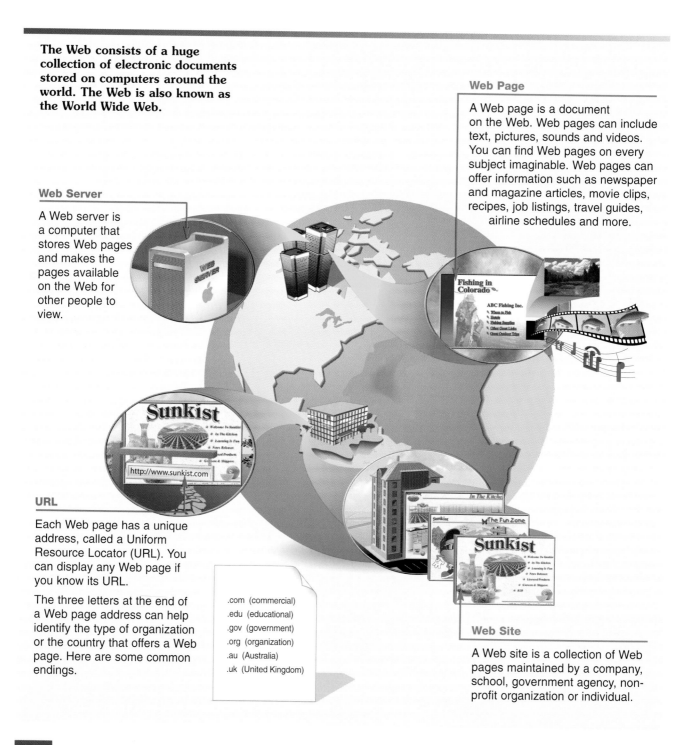

Web Page

A Web page is a document on the Web. Web pages can include text, pictures, sounds and videos. You can find Web pages on every subject imaginable. Web pages can offer information such as newspaper and magazine articles, movie clips, recipes, job listings, travel guides, airline schedules and more.

Web Server

A Web server is a computer that stores Web pages and makes the pages available on the Web for other people to view.

URL

Each Web page has a unique address, called a Uniform Resource Locator (URL). You can display any Web page if you know its URL.

The three letters at the end of a Web page address can help identify the type of organization or the country that offers a Web page. Here are some common endings.

.com (commercial)
.edu (educational)
.gov (government)
.org (organization)
.au (Australia)
.uk (United Kingdom)

Web Site

A Web site is a collection of Web pages maintained by a company, school, government agency, non-profit organization or individual.

Web Browser

A Web browser is a program that allows you to view and explore information on the Web. Mac OS X comes with the Safari™ Web browser.

Links

Web pages contain highlighted text or images, called links or hyperlinks, that connect to other pages on the Web. You can select a link to display a Web page located on the same computer or on a computer across the city, country or world.

Links allow you to easily navigate through a vast amount of information by jumping from one Web page to another, which is known as "browsing the Web."

Connecting to the Internet

You use a company called an Internet Service Provider (ISP) to connect to the Internet. Once you pay an ISP to connect to the Internet, you can view and exchange information on the Internet free of charge.

Most people connect to the Internet by using a cable modem, a Digital Subscriber Line (DSL) or a modem. A cable modem connects to the Internet using the same type of cable that attaches to a television set, while a digital subscriber line uses a high-speed digital telephone line. A modem offers the slowest type of connection and transmits information over telephone lines.

START SAFARI

You can start
Safari to browse
through pages
of information
on the Web.

START SAFARI

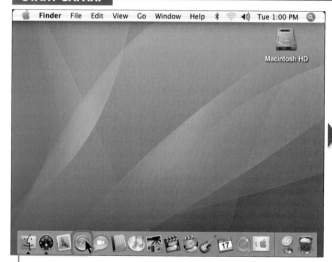

1 Click the Safari icon
to start Safari.

■ A window appears,
displaying your home
page.

*Note: Your home page is the
Web page that appears each
time you start Safari. To change
your home page, see page 258.*

2 When you finish
browsing through the
information on the Web,
you can quit Safari. Click
Safari.

3 Click **Quit Safari** to
close the Safari window.

A link connects text or an image on one Web page to another Web page. When you select the text or image, the linked Web page appears.

Links allow you to easily navigate through a vast amount of information by jumping from one Web page to another. Links are also known as hyperlinks.

SELECT A LINK

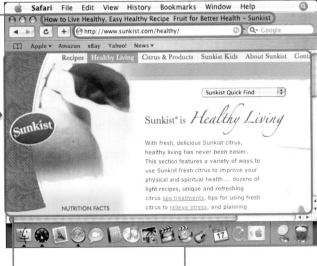

1 Position the mouse ▶ over a word or image of interest. The mouse ▶ changes to a hand 🖑 when over a link.

2 Click the word or image to display the linked Web page.

■ The linked Web page appears.

■ This area displays the title of the Web page.

■ This area displays the address of the Web page.

■ You can repeat steps **1** and **2** to continue browsing through information on the Web.

DISPLAY A SPECIFIC WEB PAGE

You can display any page on the Web that you have heard or read about.

You need to know the address of the Web page that you want to display. Each page on the Web has a unique address, called a Uniform Resource Locator (URL).

You do not need to type **http://** when typing a Web page address. For example, you do not need to type **http://** in front of www.maran.com

DISPLAY A SPECIFIC WEB PAGE

1 Click the icon in this area to highlight the current Web page address.

2 Type the address of the Web page you want to display.

■ As you type the Web page address, Safari displays a list of matching addresses. You can click an address for a Web page you want to display.

Note: If you do not want to select one of the displayed addresses, continue typing the address you want.

3 Press the return key to display the Web page.

■ The Web page appears on your screen.

If a Web page is taking a long time to appear on your screen, you can stop the transfer of the Web page.

You may also want to stop the transfer of a Web page if you realize the page contains information that does not interest you.

STOP TRANSFER OF A WEB PAGE

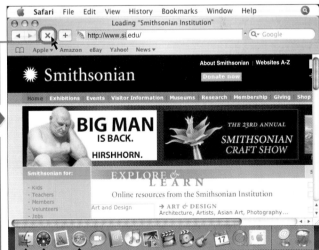

■ This area shows the progress of the transfer of a Web page to your computer.

1 Click ✕ to stop the transfer of the Web page (✕ changes to ↻).

Note: The ✕ button is available only while a Web page is transferring to your computer.

■ If you stopped the transfer of the Web page because the page was taking too long to appear, you may want to try displaying the page at a later time.

MOVE THROUGH WEB PAGES

You can easily move back and forth through the Web pages you have viewed since you last started Safari.

MOVE THROUGH WEB PAGES

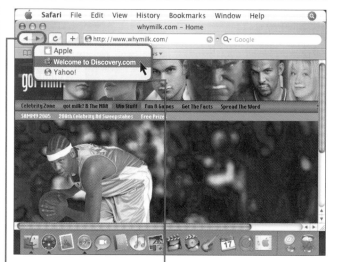

1 Click ◄ or ► to move backward or forward through the Web pages you have viewed.

Note: The ► button is only available after you use the ◄ button to return to a Web page.

■ To quickly return to the last Web page whose address you typed or whose bookmark you selected, click ⬡.

Note: For information on bookmarks, see page 264.

DISPLAY A LIST OF VIEWED WEB PAGES

1 To display a list of the Web pages you have viewed, position the mouse ▲ over ◄ or ► and then press and hold down the mouse button.

■ A list appears, displaying the names of the Web pages you have viewed.

2 Still holding down the mouse button, position the mouse ▲ over the name of the Web page you want to view again. Then release the mouse button.

BLOCK POP-UP WINDOWS

You can prevent pop-up windows from appearing when you open or close a Web page.

Some Web pages use pop-up windows to display advertisements, while other Web pages use pop-up windows to display legal information or request login information.

Keep in mind that if you block all pop-up windows, you may not see important information for some Web pages.

BLOCK POP-UP WINDOWS

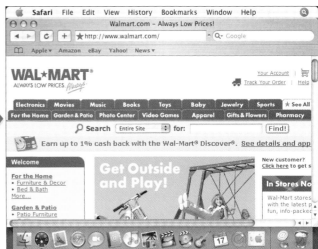

1 To prevent pop-up windows from appearing on your screen, click **Safari**.

2 Click **Block Pop-Up Windows**.

■ Pop-up windows will no longer appear when you open or close a Web page in Safari.

Note: To once again allow pop-up windows to appear, repeat steps 1 and 2.

DISPLAY AND CHANGE YOUR HOME PAGE

You can display and change the Web page that appears each time you start Safari. This page is called your home page.

DISPLAY AND CHANGE YOUR HOME PAGE

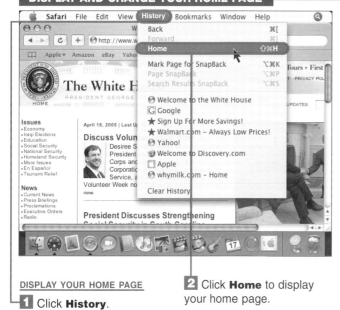

DISPLAY YOUR HOME PAGE

1 Click **History**.

2 Click **Home** to display your home page.

CHANGE YOUR HOME PAGE

1 Display the Web page you want to set as your home page.

Note: To display a specific Web page, see page 254.

2 Click **Safari**.

3 Click **Preferences**.

Tip

Which Web page should I set as my home page?

You can set any page on the Web as your home page. The page you choose should be a page you want to frequently visit. You may want to choose a page that provides a good starting point for exploring the Web, such as www.google.com, or a page that provides information relevant to your personal interests or work.

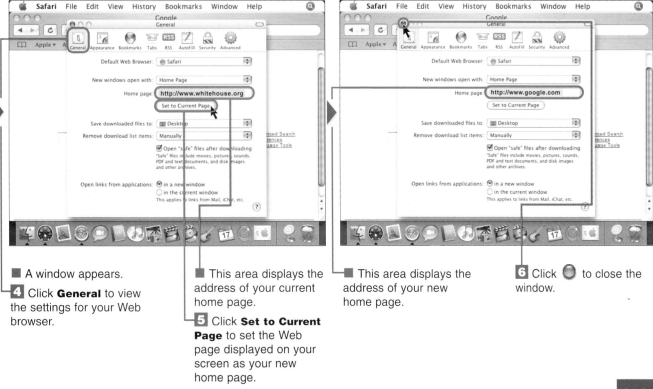

■ A window appears.

4 Click **General** to view the settings for your Web browser.

■ This area displays the address of your current home page.

5 Click **Set to Current Page** to set the Web page displayed on your screen as your new home page.

■ This area displays the address of your new home page.

6 Click ⊖ to close the window.

SEARCH THE WEB

You can search for Web pages that discuss topics of interest to you.

Safari uses the Google search engine to help you find Web pages. A search engine is a Web site that allows you to search for information on the Web.

1 Click this area and type the words that best describe the information you want to search for. Google will find Web pages that contain all the words you type.

Note: If this area contains text, drag the mouse ⌶ over the text to highlight the text. Then type the information you want to search for.

2 Press the `return` key to start the search.

■ The Google Web page appears, displaying a list of matching Web pages and their descriptions.

■ This area displays the number of matching Web pages that are currently shown and the total number of matching Web pages.

3 To display a Web page of interest, click the title of the Web page.

Tip

How can I narrow my search and find more relevant results?

To narrow your search, use specific rather than general words whenever possible. For example, if you want to find Web pages about porsches, type **porsche** instead of **car**.

You can also use quotation marks ("") to find words that are side-by-side on a Web page. For example, if you are searching for Thomas Edison, surround the name in quotation marks (example, "Thomas Edison") to ensure that Google will find only Web pages that contain the entire name.

■ The Web page you selected appears.

■ You can click ◐ in this area to return to the list of Web pages and select another Web page.

REPEAT A PREVIOUS SEARCH

1 To quickly repeat a search you previously performed, click **Q▼** in this area to display a list of your previous search terms.

2 Click the search term for the search you want to repeat.

DISPLAY HISTORY OF VIEWED WEB PAGES

Safari uses the History list to keep track of the Web pages you have recently viewed. You can display the History list at any time to redisplay a Web page.

The History list keeps track of the Web pages you have viewed in the past week.

DISPLAY RECENTLY VIEWED PAGES

1 Click **History** to display a list of the Web pages you have recently viewed.

■ This area displays the Web pages you have recently viewed.

2 Click the Web page you want to view.

■ The Web page you selected appears.

Can I erase the list of Web pages I have recently viewed?

Yes. You can clear the History list to erase the list of Web pages you have recently viewed.

1 Click **History**.

2 Click **Clear History** to clear your History list.

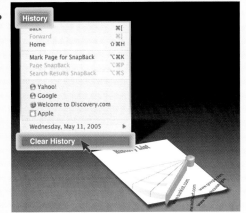

DISPLAY PAGES FROM ANOTHER DAY

1 Click **History** to display the History list.

2 To display a list of the Web pages you viewed earlier today or on a specific day, position the mouse ► over the day you want in this area.

■ A list of Web pages you viewed on the day you selected appear.

3 Click the Web page you want to view.

■ The Web page you selected appears.

CREATE A BOOKMARK

You can use the
Bookmarks feature
to create a list of
Web pages you
frequently visit. The
Bookmarks feature
allows you to
quickly display a
favorite Web page
at any time.

Selecting Web
pages from your list
of bookmarks saves
you from having to
remember and
constantly retype
the same Web
page addresses.

You can store a
bookmark on the
Bookmarks Bar at
the top of your
screen or in one of
the many bookmarks
folders Safari
provides.

CREATE A BOOKMARK

1 Display the Web
page you want to
add to your list of
bookmarks.

*Note: To display a specific
Web page, see page 254.*

2 Click ⊞.

■ A dialog sheet
appears.

■ This area displays the
name of the Web page.
To use a different name
for your bookmark, type
the name.

■ This area displays the
location where the
bookmark will be stored.
You can click this area to
specify a different location.

3 Click **Add** to add the
bookmark to your list of
favorite Web pages.

Does Safari automatically create bookmarks for me?

Yes. Safari automatically creates bookmarks for several popular Web pages and creates folders to help organize all the bookmarks. You can use bookmarks created by Safari the same way you use bookmarks you add yourself.

How do I remove a bookmark?

To remove a Web page from your list of bookmarks, click 🕮 to display all your bookmarks. Click the bookmark you want to remove and then press the delete key. Removing bookmarks you no longer visit can help keep your bookmarks list from becoming cluttered.

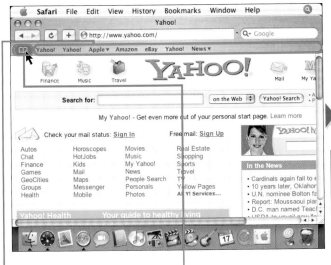

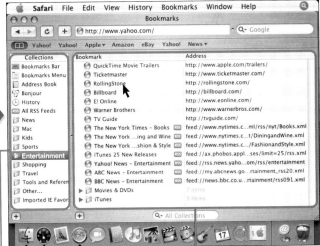

USING BOOKMARKS

■ This area displays the names of bookmarks that have been added to the Bookmarks Bar. You can click the name of a bookmark to quickly display the Web page.

1 To view all your bookmarks, click 🕮 .

■ Your bookmarks appear.

■ This area displays folders for all your bookmark collections.

2 To view the bookmarks in a folder, click the name of the folder.

■ The bookmarks in the folder appear in this area.

3 To display a Web page, double-click its bookmark in this area.

USING SHERLOCK

You can use Sherlock to search for information of interest on the Internet. Sherlock helps you locate information such as Web sites, flight information, movies schedules and much more.

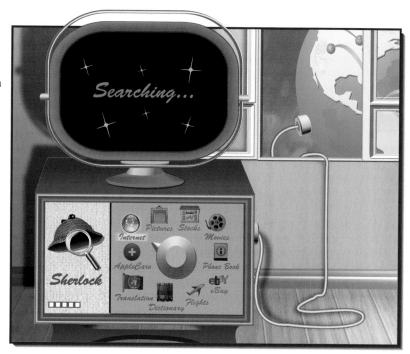

USING SHERLOCK

1 Click **Go**.

Note: If Go is not available, click a blank area on your desktop to display the Finder menu bar.

2 Click **Applications** to view the applications available on your computer.

■ The Applications window appears.

3 Double-click **Sherlock** to start Sherlock.

■ The Sherlock window appears.

Tip

What collections of channels does Sherlock provide?

Sherlock includes several collections of channels you can use to search for information.

Toolbar and Channels Menu

The Toolbar and Channels Menu collections contain the most commonly used channels. Each channel in the Toolbar collection appears on the Sherlock toolbar. Each channel in the Channels Menu collection appears in the Channel menu.

Apple Channels

The Apple Channels collection contains many of the same channels as the Toolbar and Channels Menu collections, but also includes some specialized channels, such as a Japanese news channel.

Other Channels

The Other Channels collection contains a wide variety of channels from around the world.

*Note: The first time you view the Other Channels collection, a dialog sheet appears. Click **Proceed** to continue.*

My Channels

The My Channels collection allows you to create a personalized list of the channels you use most often. You can drag a channel of interest from any collection to the My Channels collection to add the channel to the collection.

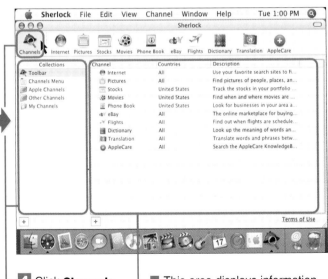

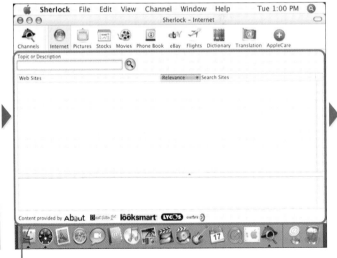

4 Click **Channels**.

■ This area displays the available collections of channels. You can click a collection of interest to view the channels in the collection.

■ This area displays information about the channels available in the selected collection.

5 Double-click a channel in this area to display the channel.

Note: The available collections and channels may change at any time. The channels displayed above may be different than the channels displayed on your screen.

■ The channel appears in this area.

*Note: The following steps depend on the channel you selected in step 5. In this example, we selected **Internet** in step 5.*

CONTINUED

USING SHERLOCK

Each channel you select allows you to enter information about the item you want to find. Sherlock will then search the Internet to find the item for you.

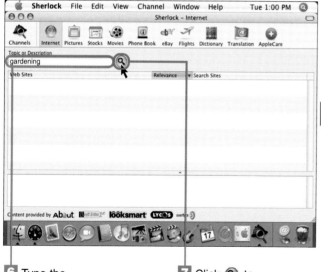

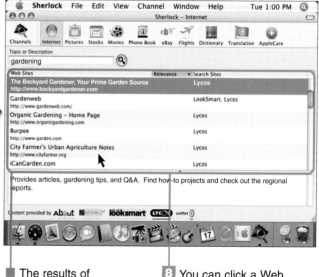

6 Type the information you want to find in the channel.

7 Click 🔍 to start the search.

■ The results of your search appear.

■ In this example, a list of Web pages about gardening appears.

8 You can click a Web page of interest to view a description of the Web page.

Tip

What types of information can I search for using Sherlock?

Sherlock offers many channels that allow you to search for specific types of information. The following channels are available in the Toolbar collection. You can click a button on the toolbar at any time to display the channel and search for information.

Web pages	Goods and services on eBay
Pictures on the Internet	Flight information
Stock market information	Dictionary definitions
Movies playing locally	Translation of text you specify
Location of a business	Help documents in the AppleCare Knowledge Base

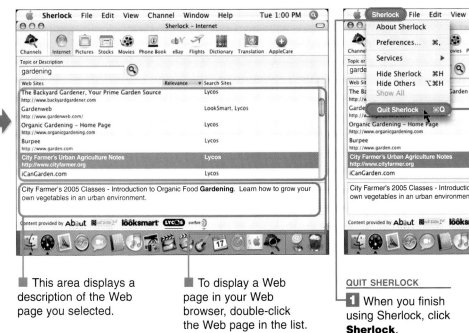

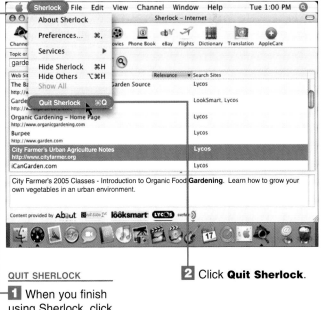

■ This area displays a description of the Web page you selected.

■ To display a Web page in your Web browser, double-click the Web page in the list.

QUIT SHERLOCK

1 When you finish using Sherlock, click **Sherlock**.

2 Click **Quit Sherlock**.

CHAPTER 12

Exchange E-mail

The Mail program allows you to exchange e-mail messages with people around the world. In this chapter, you will learn how to read, send and work with e-mail messages.

READ MESSAGES

You can start Mail to open and read the contents of your e-mail messages.

The first time you start Mail, a dialog box will appear if you have not yet set up your e-mail account. Follow the instructions in the dialog box to set up your e-mail account.

READ MESSAGES

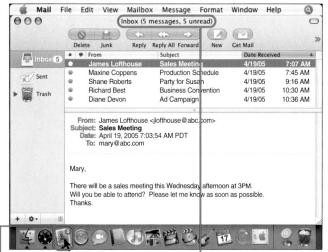

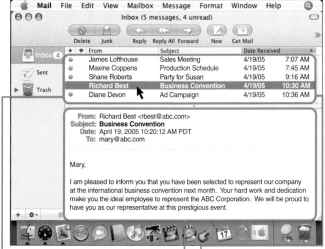

START MAIL

1 Click the Mail icon to start Mail.

■ A window appears, displaying the messages in the current mailbox.

■ This area displays the name of the current mailbox. The total number of messages and the number of unread messages in the mailbox appear in brackets beside the mailbox name.

READ MESSAGES

■ This area displays the messages in the current mailbox. Unread messages display a dot (●).

Note: Messages considered to be junk mail appear brown in color. For information on junk mail, see page 288.

1 Click the message you want to read.

■ This area displays the contents of the message you selected.

■ To display the contents of another message, repeat step **1**.

What mailboxes does Mail use to store my messages?

 Inbox	Stores messages sent to you.
Outbox	Temporarily stores messages that have not yet been sent.
Drafts	Stores messages you have not yet completed.
Sent	Stores copies of messages you have sent.
Trash	Stores messages you have deleted.

Note: Mail creates the Drafts mailbox the first time you save a message you have not yet completed. Mail creates the Trash mailbox the first time you delete a message.

Does Mail block pictures in my e-mail messages?

Mail can block pictures from displaying in your messages to help you avoid viewing potentially offensive material. When Mail blocks pictures in a message, a blue square ( ) appears in place of each blocked picture. If a message is from a reliable source and you want to view the blocked picture, click **Load Images** at the top of the message.

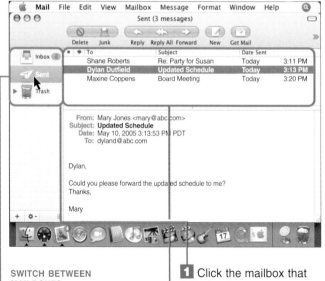

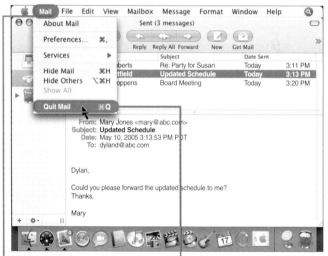

SWITCH BETWEEN MAILBOXES

■ This area displays a list of mailboxes.

Note: A circled number beside a mailbox name indicates how many unread messages the folder contains. The number disappears when you have read all the messages in the folder.

1 Click the mailbox that contains the messages you want to view.

■ The messages in the mailbox you selected appear in this area.

QUIT MAIL

1 When you finish reading your e-mail messages, click **Mail**.

2 Click **Quit Mail** to close the Mail window.

SEND A MESSAGE

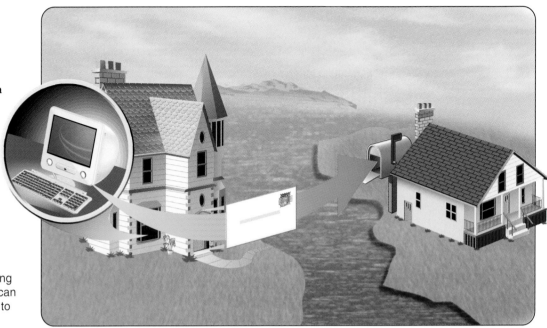

You can send
a message to
express an idea
or request
information.

To practice sending
a message, you can
send a message to
yourself.

SEND A MESSAGE

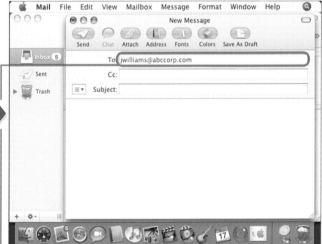

1 Click **New** to create
a new message.

■ The New Message
window appears.

2 Type the e-mail
address of the person
you want to receive
the message.

*Note: If you start typing the
name or e-mail address of a
person in Address Book, Mail
will automatically complete the
person's e-mail address for
you. Press the* `return` *key to
accept Mail's suggestion. To
add a person to Address Book,
see page 124.*

Tip

How can I express emotions in my e-mail messages?

You can use special characters, called smileys, to express emotions in e-mail messages. These characters resemble human faces if you turn them sideways.

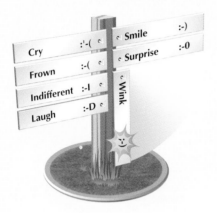

 Tip

Can Mail help me correct a spelling error in a message?

Yes. To get help correcting a spelling error in a message, press and hold down the control key as you click the misspelled word. A menu appears, displaying suggestions to correct the spelling error. Click the suggestion you want to use to correct the spelling error.

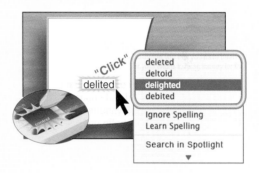

3 To send a copy of the message to a person who is not directly involved but would be interested in the message, click this area and then type the person's e-mail address.

Note: To send the message to more than one person in step 2 or 3, separate each e-mail address with a comma (,).

4 Click this area and then type the subject of the message.

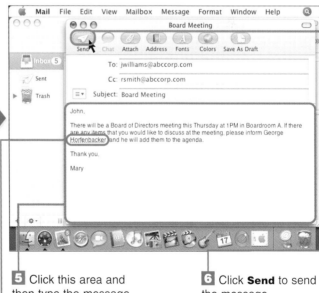

5 Click this area and then type the message.

■ Mail checks your spelling as you type and displays a dotted red underline under potential spelling errors. The person who receives the message will not see the dotted red underlines.

6 Click **Send** to send the message.

■ Mail sends the message and stores a copy of the message in the Sent mailbox.

SAVE A DRAFT OF A MESSAGE

You can save a draft of a message so you can send the message at a later time.

Saving a draft of a message allows you to later review and make changes to a message.

SAVE A DRAFT OF A MESSAGE

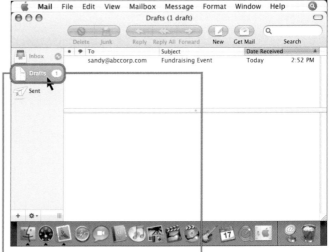

1 To create a message, perform steps **1** to **5** starting on page 274.

2 Click **Save As Draft** to save the message as a draft so you can send the message at a later time.

3 Click ⬤ to close the message window.

SEND A DRAFT MESSAGE

■ When you save a draft of a message, Mail stores the message in the Drafts mailbox until you are ready to send the message.

1 Click **Drafts** to display the messages in the Drafts mailbox.

I am still not ready to send a draft message. What should I do?

While reviewing a message you have saved as a draft, you can once again save the message so you can send the message at a later time. You can review a draft message as many times as you need until you are happy with the contents of the message. To save changes you have made to a draft message and close the message window, repeat steps 2 and 3 on page 276.

I no longer want to send a message I saved as a draft. How can I delete the message?

If you no longer want to send a message you saved as a draft, you can delete the message from the Drafts mailbox as you would delete any message. To delete a message, see page 285.

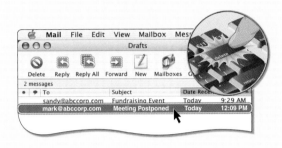

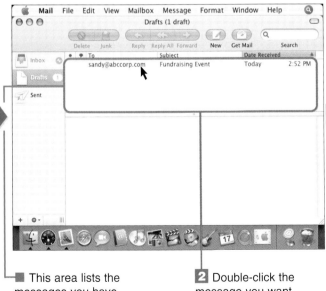

■ This area lists the messages you have saved as drafts.

2 Double-click the message you want to send.

■ A window appears, displaying the contents of the message. You can review and make changes to the message.

3 To send the message, click **Send**.

■ Mail removes the message from the Drafts mailbox and places a copy of the message in the Sent mailbox.

REPLY TO A MESSAGE

You can reply to a message to answer a question, express an opinion or supply additional information.

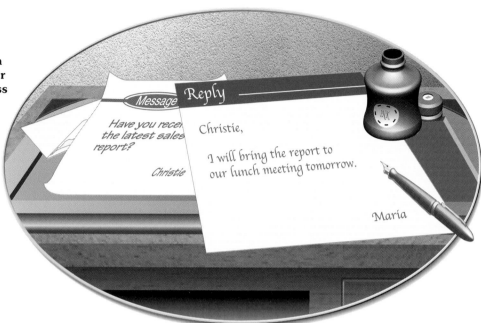

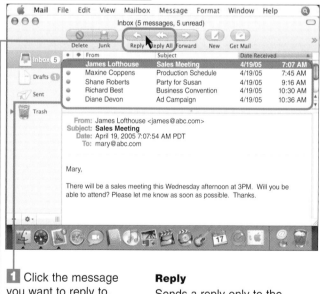

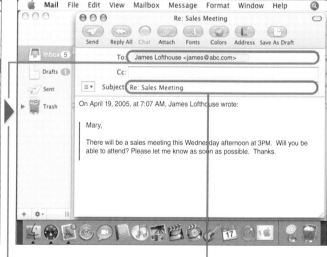

1 Click the message you want to reply to.

2 Click the reply option you want to use.

Reply

Sends a reply only to the author.

Reply All

Sends a reply to the author and everyone who received the original message.

■ A window appears for you to compose your reply.

■ Mail fills in the e-mail address(es) for you.

■ Mail also fills in the subject, starting the subject with **Re:**.

How can I save time when typing a message?

You can use abbreviations for words and phrases to save time when typing messages. Here are some commonly used abbreviations.

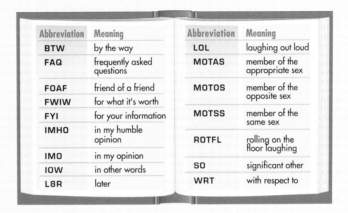

Abbreviation	Meaning
BTW	by the way
FAQ	frequently asked questions
FOAF	friend of a friend
FWIW	for what it's worth
FYI	for your information
IMHO	in my humble opinion
IMO	in my opinion
IOW	in other words
L8R	later

Abbreviation	Meaning
LOL	laughing out loud
MOTAS	member of the appropriate sex
MOTOS	member of the opposite sex
MOTSS	member of the same sex
ROTFL	rolling on the floor laughing
SO	significant other
WRT	with respect to

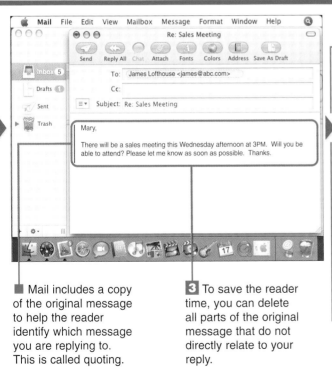

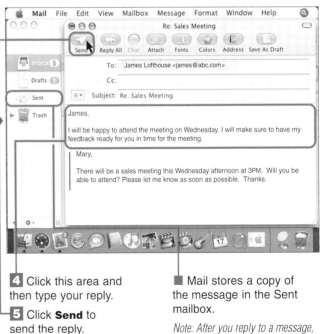

■ Mail includes a copy of the original message to help the reader identify which message you are replying to. This is called quoting.

3 To save the reader time, you can delete all parts of the original message that do not directly relate to your reply.

4 Click this area and then type your reply.

5 Click **Send** to send the reply.

■ Mail stores a copy of the message in the Sent mailbox.

Note: After you reply to a message, Mail displays a curved arrow (↰) beside the original message in the mailbox.

FORWARD A MESSAGE

After reading a message, you can add comments and then forward the message to a friend, family member or colleague.

Forwarding a message is useful when you know another person would be interested in a message.

FORWARD A MESSAGE

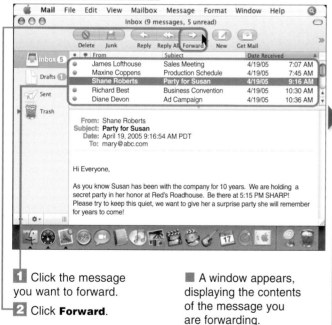

1 Click the message you want to forward.

2 Click **Forward**.

■ A window appears, displaying the contents of the message you are forwarding.

3 Type the e-mail address of the person you want to receive the message.

■ Mail fills in the subject for you, starting the subject with **Fwd:**.

4 Click this area and then type any comments about the message you are forwarding.

5 Click **Send** to send the message.

Note: After you forward a message, Mail displays an arrow (→) beside the original message in the mailbox.

If you are waiting for an important message, you can have Mail immediately check for new mail.

You can also change how often Mail checks for new mail. Mail initially checks for new mail every 5 minutes when you are connected to the Internet.

CHECK FOR NEW MAIL

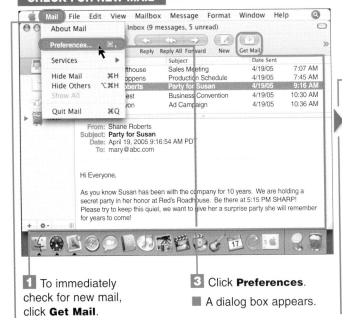

1 To immediately check for new mail, click **Get Mail**.

2 To change how often Mail checks for new mail, click **Mail**.

3 Click **Preferences**.

■ A dialog box appears.

4 Click **General** to change how Mail works.

5 This area displays how often Mail checks for new mail. To change how often Mail checks for new mail, click this area.

6 Click an option to specify how often you want Mail to check for new mail.

7 Click ⬤ to confirm your change.

ATTACH A FILE TO A MESSAGE

You can attach a file to a message you are sending. Attaching a file to a message is useful when you want to include additional information with the message.

You can attach many types of files to a message, including documents, photos, videos and sounds. The computer receiving the message must have the necessary software installed to display or play the file you attach.

ATTACH A FILE TO A MESSAGE

1 To create a message, perform steps **1** to **5** starting on page 274.

2 Click **Attach** to attach a file to the message.

■ A dialog sheet appears.

■ This area shows the location of the displayed files. You can click this area to change the location.

3 Click the name of the file you want to attach to the message.

■ This area displays information about the file you selected.

4 Click **Choose File** to attach the file to the message.

Tip

Can I attach a large file to a message?

The company that provides your e-mail account will usually limit the size of the messages that you can send and receive over the Internet. Most companies do not allow you to send or receive messages larger than 10 MB, which includes all attached files.

Tip

How can I remove a file I accidentally attached to a message?

To remove a file you accidentally attached to a message, click the icon for the file you want to remove and then press the `delete` key. The file disappears from the message.

Note: To remove a picture, click the picture in the message and then press the `delete` key.

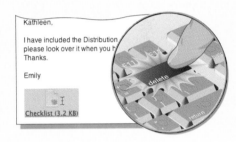

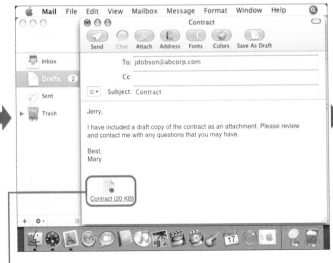

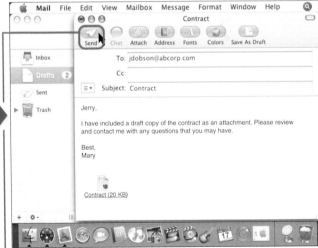

■ An icon for the file appears in the message.

Note: If you attached a picture to the message, the picture appears in the message.

■ To attach additional files to the message, perform steps **2** to **4** for each file you want to attach.

5 Click **Send** to send the message.

■ Mail sends the message and the attached file(s) to the e-mail address(es) you specified. Mail also stores a copy of the message in the Sent mailbox.

VIEW AN ATTACHED FILE

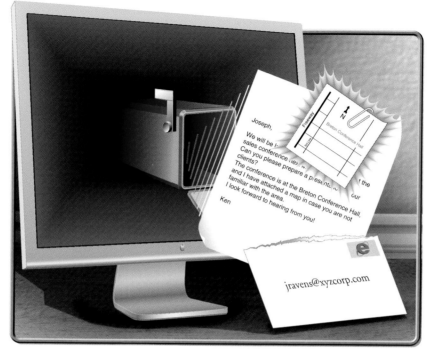

You can easily view a file attached to a message you receive.

Before viewing an attached file, make sure the file is from a reliable source. Some files can contain viruses, which can damage the information on your computer.

VIEW AN ATTACHED FILE

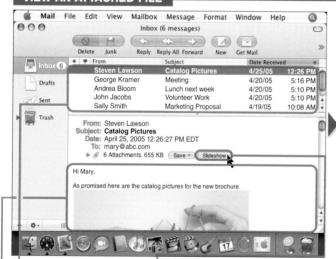

1 Click a message with an attached file.

■ Pictures attached to the message appear in this area.

Note: Other files, such as documents, appear as links at the bottom of the message. To open a file, click the link for the file.

2 To view a slideshow of all the pictures attached to the message, click **Slideshow**.

■ A slideshow of all the pictures attached to the message begins.

3 To end the slideshow at any time, move the mouse ▶ on your screen. A toolbar appears.

4 Click ⊗ to end the slideshow and return to the Mail window.

DELETE A MESSAGE

You can delete a message you no longer need. Deleting messages prevents your mailboxes from becoming cluttered with messages.

DELETE A MESSAGE

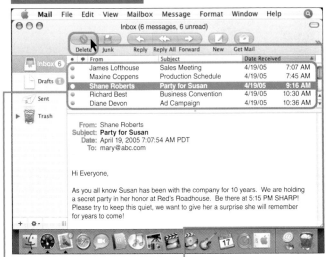

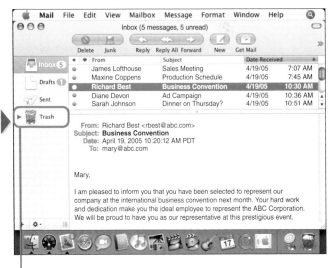

1 Click the message you want to delete.

2 Click **Delete** to delete the message.

■ Mail removes the message from the current mailbox and places the message in the Trash mailbox.

Note: Deleting a message from the Trash mailbox will permanently remove the message from your computer. To view the contents of the Trash mailbox, see page 272.

SELECT A NAME FROM ADDRESS BOOK

When sending a message, you can select the name of the person you want to receive the message from Address Book.

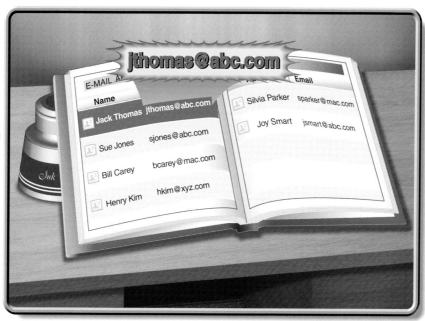

jthomas@abc.com

Address Book allows you to store information about people you frequently contact. To send a message to a person in Address Book, you must have entered an e-mail address for the person in Address Book. To add a person to Address Book, see page 124.

SELECT A NAME FROM ADDRESS BOOK

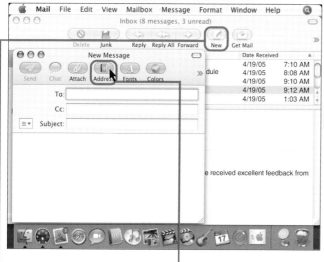

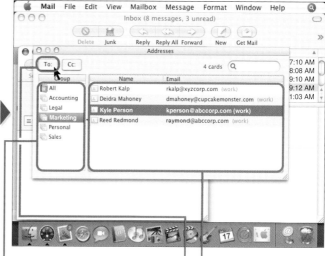

1 Click **New** to create a new message.

■ The New Message window appears.

2 Click **Address** to select a name from Address Book.

■ The Addresses window appears.

3 Click the group that contains the person you want to receive the message.

■ To send the message to every person in a group, click the group and then skip to step **5**.

Note: The All group contains all the people you have added to Address Book.

4 Click the name of the person you want to receive the message.

5 Click **To:**.

■ You can repeat steps **4** and **5** for each person you want to receive the message.

I accidentally selected a name from Address Book. How can I remove the name from the message?

To remove the name of a person you accidentally selected from Address Book, you must first select the name. If the person's name and e-mail address appear, drag the mouse ⌶ over the information until the information is highlighted. If the person's name appears in a blue oval, click the oval to select the oval. Press the delete key to remove the information you selected.

The person I want to select does not appear in Address Book. How can I quickly add the person to Address Book?

You can quickly add the name and e-mail address of a person who sent you an e-mail message to Address Book. Click a message you received from the person you want to add to Address Book and then press and hold down the ⌘ key as you press the Y key. The person's name and e-mail address will now appear in Address Book.

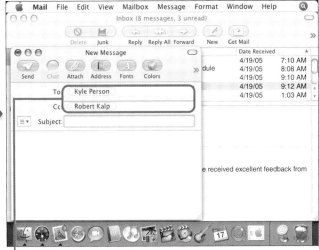

6 To send a copy of the message to a person who is not directly involved but would be interested in the message, click the name of the person.

7 Click **Cc:**.

■ You can repeat steps **6** and **7** for each person you want to receive a copy of the message.

8 When you finish selecting names from Address Book, click ● to close the Addresses window.

■ This area displays the name of each person you selected from Address Book. The name may appear in a blue oval or may include the person's e-mail address.

■ You can now finish composing the message.

Note: To finish composing a message, perform steps 4 to 6 on page 275.

SORT JUNK MAIL

Mail can examine messages you receive to determine if the messages are junk mail.

By default, Mail changes the color of potential junk e-mail messages to brown so you can easily recognize junk mail when reading your messages.

You can mark messages as junk mail to help Mail learn how to identify junk e-mail. You can also have Mail automatically move new junk mail you receive to the Junk mailbox.

SORT JUNK MAIL

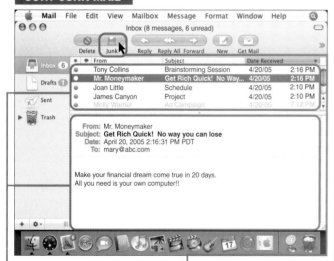

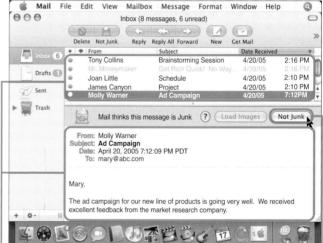

MARK A MESSAGE AS JUNK MAIL

1 Click the message you want to mark as junk mail.

■ This area displays the contents of the message.

2 Click **Junk**.

■ The message will appear brown in color.

Note: The first time you mark a message as junk mail, a dialog box appears, providing information about junk mail. To close the dialog box, click OK.

MARK A MESSAGE AS NOT JUNK MAIL

1 Click the message that Mail incorrectly identified as junk mail.

■ This area displays the contents of the message.

Note: A bar appears at the top of the message, indicating that Mail thinks the message is junk mail.

2 Click **Not Junk**.

■ The message will no longer appear brown in color.

Can I stop Mail from identifying and sorting junk mail?

Yes. You can turn off the junk mail feature to stop Mail from automatically identifying and sorting junk mail. To turn off the junk mail feature, perform steps **1** to **3** on page 289 to access your Mail preferences. Click **Enable Junk Mail filtering** to turn off the junk mail feature (☑ changes to ☐).

Can I permanently erase the contents of the Junk mailbox?

Yes. You can erase the contents of the Junk mailbox to delete all the junk e-mail messages it contains from your computer. Click the **Mailbox** menu and then click **Erase Junk Mail**. In the confirmation dialog box that appears, click **Yes** to erase all the junk mail in your Junk mailbox.

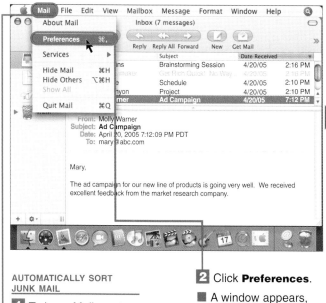

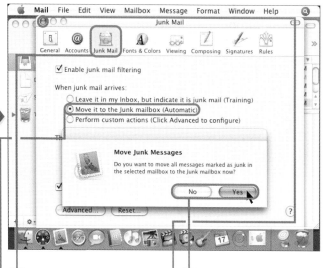

AUTOMATICALLY SORT JUNK MAIL

1 To have Mail create a Junk mailbox and automatically move junk mail to the Junk mailbox, click **Mail**.

2 Click **Preferences**.

■ A window appears, allowing you to change your Mail preferences.

3 Click **Junk Mail** to change your junk mail preferences.

4 Click this option to have Mail automatically move junk mail to the Junk mailbox (○ changes to ●).

5 A dialog box appears, asking if you want to move all junk e-mail messages to the Junk mailbox now. Click **Yes** or **No** to continue.

6 Click ● to close the window.

CHAPTER 13

Exchange Instant Messages

You can use iChat to exchange instant messages with your friends and family. This chapter shows you how to add a person to your Buddy List, send an instant message and send a file.

START iCHAT

You can use iChat to see when your friends are available and exchange instant messages and files with them.

START iCHAT

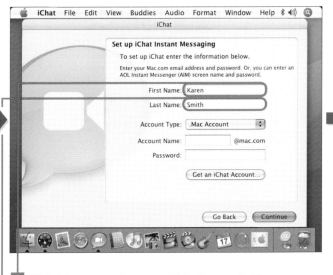

1 Click the iChat icon to start iChat.

■ The first time you start iChat, the iChat dialog box appears, allowing you to set up iChat.

2 Click **Continue**.

3 Click this area and type your first name.

4 Click this area and type your last name.

Note: Some or all of the information in the dialog box may already be filled in for you. To change existing information, drag the mouse I over the information until the information is highlighted. Then type the new information.

Tip

How do I obtain an account that I can use with iChat?

.Mac Account

You can use a .Mac account with iChat. If you do not have a .Mac account, click **Get an iChat Account** in the iChat dialog box. Your Web browser opens, displaying a Web page that allows you to obtain a .Mac account.

AIM Account

If you use the AIM (AOL Instant Messenger) application, you can use the screen name and password for your AIM account with iChat. If you use AOL (America Online) to access the Internet, you can use the screen name and password for your AOL account with iChat.

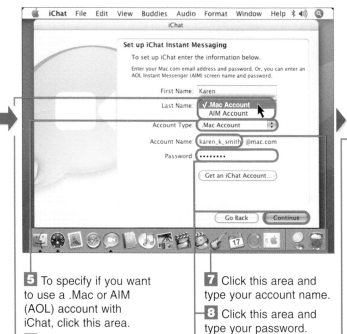

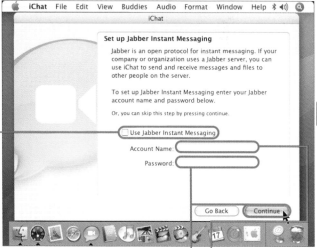

5 To specify if you want to use a .Mac or AIM (AOL) account with iChat, click this area.

6 Click the type of account you want to use.

7 Click this area and type your account name.

8 Click this area and type your password.

9 Click **Continue**.

■ If your company or organization uses a Jabber server, Jabber Instant Messaging allows you to exchange messages with other people on the server.

Note: If you do not want to use Jabber Instant Messaging, skip to step 13.

10 Click this option to use Jabber Instant Messaging (☐ changes to ☑).

11 Click this area and type your Jabber account name.

12 Click this area and type your Jabber password.

13 Click **Continue**.

CONTINUED

START iCHAT

You can use iChat to talk to another person over the Internet. You can also view live video of the other person during a conversation.

Using iChat to talk to other people over the Internet allows you to avoid long-distance telephone charges.

START iCHAT (CONTINUED)

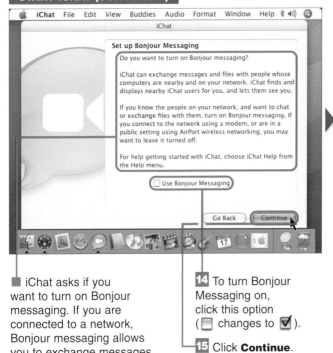

■ iChat asks if you want to turn on Bonjour messaging. If you are connected to a network, Bonjour messaging allows you to exchange messages with other people using iChat on the network.

14 To turn Bonjour Messaging on, click this option (☐ changes to ☑).

15 Click **Continue**.

■ If your video camera is attached to the computer and turned on, this area displays the video area another person will see on their screen during a video chat.

Note: If your computer does not support video chat, skip to step 17.

16 Position your camera until this area displays the video area you want other people to see.

17 Click **Continue**.

Tip

What hardware and software do I need to set up iChat for video chat?

To participate in a video chat with another person, your computer and the other person's computer must both be Macintosh G4 computers or G3 computers with at least a 600 MHz processor. Both your computer and the other person's computer must also have a video camera connected using a FireWire connection.

G4 600 MHz

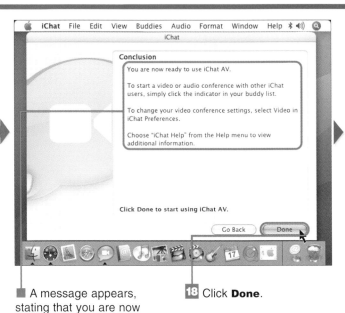

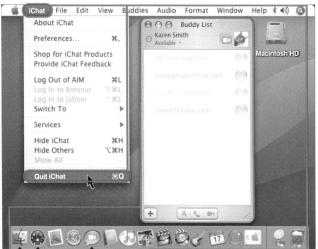

■ A message appears, stating that you are now ready to use iChat.

18 Click **Done**.

■ The Buddy List window appears. You can add people to your Buddy List so you can quickly send them instant messages.

Note: To add a person to your Buddy List, see page 296.

■ If you chose to turn on Bonjour messaging in step **14**, the Bonjour window also appears on your screen.

19 When you finish using iChat, click **iChat**.

20 Click **Quit iChat**.

ADD A PERSON TO YOUR BUDDY LIST

You can add a
person to your
Buddy List so
you can see
when the person
is available to
exchange instant
messages.

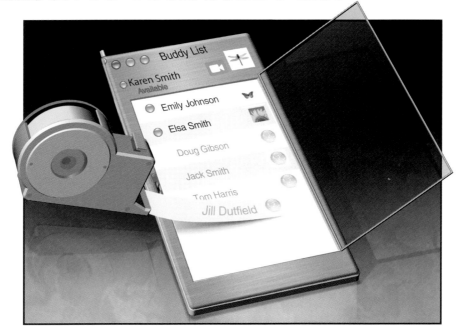

ADD A PERSON TO YOUR BUDDY LIST

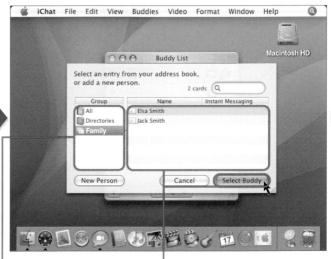

1 Click the iChat icon to
start iChat.

■ The Buddy List window
appears, displaying each
person you have added to
your Buddy List.

■ Each person who
is available displays
a green dot (●).
Each person who is
not available appears
dim or displays a red
dot (●).

2 Click ✚ to add
a person to your
Buddy List.

■ A dialog sheet
appears, listing the
people in Address
Book.

*Note: For information on
Address Book, see page 124.*

3 Click the group that
contains the person
you want to add to
your Buddy List.

*Note: The All group contains
all the people in Address Book.*

4 Click the person you
want to add to your
Buddy List.

*Note: If the person you want to
add is not listed, see the top of
page 297.*

5 Click **Select Buddy**.

Tip

Can I add a person who is not listed in Address Book to my Buddy List?

Yes. Click ➕ in the Buddy List window. In the dialog sheet that appears, click **New Person** and then perform steps **6** to **8** below. You can also enter the person's first name, last name and e-mail address to provide additional information for Address Book. Click **Add** to add the person to your Buddy List and to Address Book.

 Tip

How do I remove a person from my Buddy List?

In the Buddy List window, click the name of the person you want to remove and then press the `delete` key. In the confirmation dialog sheet that appears, click **Delete** to delete the person from your Buddy List.

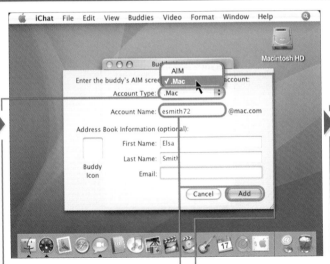

■ If Address Book does not contain an instant message account for the person, a dialog sheet appears, asking you to enter the person's account name.

6 Click this area to select the type of account the person uses.

7 Click an option to specify if the person uses a .Mac account or an AIM (AOL) account.

8 Click this area and type the person's account name.

9 Click **Add** to add the person to your Buddy List.

■ The person appears in your Buddy List.

SEND AN INSTANT MESSAGE

You can send an instant message to a person in your Buddy List.

When sending instant messages, never give out your password or credit card information.

SEND AN INSTANT MESSAGE

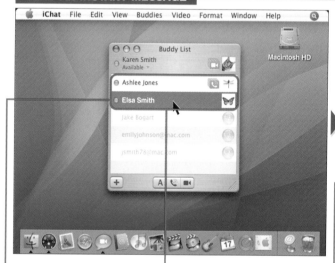

■ You can send an instant message to a person in your Buddy List who is available. A green dot (●) appears beside the name of each person who is available.

Note: To add a person to your Buddy List, see page 296.

1 Double-click the name of a person you want to send an instant message to.

■ A chat window appears.

2 Click this area and type your message.

Note: To start a new paragraph while typing a message, press and hold down the `option` *key as you press the* `return` *key.*

3 To express an emotion in your message, click ☺.

4 Click the smiley you want to include in your message.

5 To send the message, press the `return` key.

Tip

How can I start a video chat with another person in my Buddy List?

Both computers must support video and audio conferencing in iChat to start a video chat.

Note: When the other person accepts your invitation to video chat, the other person's image appears on your screen.

■ **1** Click the name of the person you want to video chat with.

■ **2** Click ▣ to start a video chat.

■ A preview window appears, displaying what the other person will view on their screen.

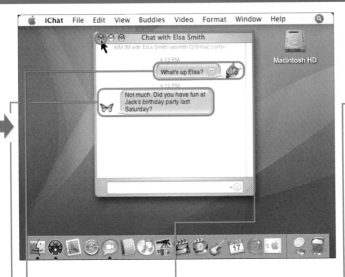

■ This area displays the message you sent.

■ The other person's response appears below the message you sent.

Note: While you or the other person type a message, a new icon with an empty balloon appears in the chat window.

■ **6** When you finish exchanging instant messages, click ◯ to close the chat window.

RECEIVE AN INSTANT MESSAGE

■ When you receive an instant message that is not part of an ongoing conversation, a window appears, displaying the message.

■ **1** To respond to the message, click anywhere in the window.

■ An area appears, allowing you to type a reply.

■ **2** Click this area and type your reply. Then press the `return` key.

SEND A FILE

While exchanging instant messages with another person, you can send the person a file.

You can send many types of files, including documents, pictures, videos and sounds. The computer receiving the file must have the necessary software installed to display or play the file.

There is no limit on the size of files you can send in your instant messages, but larger files will take longer to transfer.

SEND A FILE

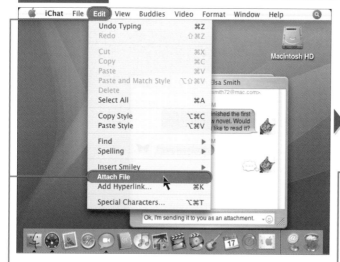

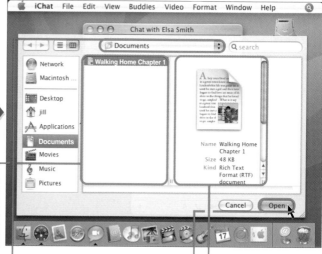

1 While exchanging instant messages with another person, click **Edit**.

2 Click **Attach File** to send a file.

Note: For information on sending instant messages, see page 298.

■ A dialog sheet appears.

■ This area shows the location of the displayed files. You can click this area to change the location.

3 Click the name of the file you want to send.

■ Information about the file appears in this area.

4 Click **Open** to select the file.

How do I accept a file I receive?

To accept a file you receive, click the name of the file in the chat window. After Mac OS X transfers the file to your computer, the Desktop window appears, displaying an icon for the file. You can double-click the icon to open the file. An icon for the file also appears on your desktop.

Is there another way to send a file?

Yes. To quickly send a file, click the area where you type your instant messages. Position the mouse ▶ over the file you want to send and then drag the file into the area. An icon for the file appears in the area. To send the file, press the return key.

■ An icon for the file appears in this area.

5 To send the file, press the return key.

■ A dialog box appears on your screen until the other person accepts the file.

■ To cancel the file transfer at any time, click **Stop**.

Note: If you send a picture, the picture may automatically appear in the chat window without displaying a dialog box.

INDEX

INDEX

INDEX

INDEX

GUITAR

MARAN ILLUSTRATED™ Guitar is an excellent resource for people who want to learn to play the guitar, as well as for current musicians who want to fine tune their technique. This full-color guide includes over 500 photographs, accompanied by step-by-step instructions that teach you the basics of playing the guitar and reading music, as well as advanced guitar techniques. You will also learn what to look for when purchasing a guitar or accessories, how to maintain and repair your guitar and much more.

Whether you want to learn to strum your favorite tunes or play professionally, MARAN ILLUSTRATED™ Guitar provides all the information you need to become a proficient guitarist.

BOOK BONUS!

Visit **www.maran.com/guitar** to download MP3 files you can listen to and play along with for all the chords, scales, exercises and practice pieces in the book.

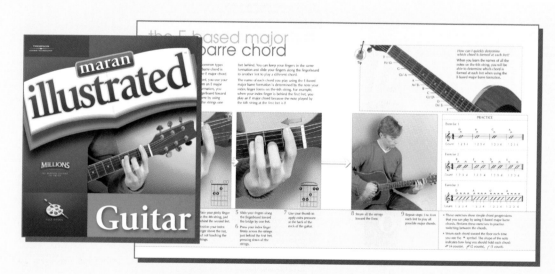

ISBN: 1-59200-860-7
Price: $24.99 US; $33.95 CDN
Page count: 320

PIANO

MARAN ILLUSTRATED™ Piano is an information-packed resource for people who want to learn to play the piano, as well as current musicians looking to hone their skills. Combining full-color photographs and easy-to-follow instructions, this guide covers everything from the basics of piano playing to more advanced techniques. Not only does MARAN ILLUSTRATED™ Piano show you how to read music, play scales and chords and improvise while playing with other musicians, it also provides you with helpful information for purchasing and caring for your piano. You will also learn what to look for when you buy a piano or piano accessories, how to find the best location for your piano and how to clean your piano.

ISBN: 1-59200-864-X

Price: $24.99 US; $33.95 CDN

Page count: 304

DOG TRAINING

MARAN ILLUSTRATED™ Dog Training is an excellent guide for both current dog owners and people considering making a dog part of their family. Using clear, step-by-step instructions accompanied by over 400 full-color photographs, MARAN ILLUSTRATED™ Dog Training is perfect for any visual learner who prefers seeing what to do rather than reading lengthy explanations.

Beginning with insights into popular dog breeds and puppy development, this book emphasizes positive training methods to guide you through socializing, housetraining and teaching your dog many commands. You will also learn how to work with problem behaviors, such as destructive chewing, excessive barking and separation anxiety.

ISBN: 1-59200-858-5
Price: $19.99 US; $26.95 CDN
Page count: 256

KNITTING & CROCHETING

MARAN ILLUSTRATED™ Knitting & Crocheting contains a wealth of information about these two increasingly popular crafts. Whether you are just starting out or you are an experienced knitter or crocheter interested in picking up new tips and techniques, this information-packed resource will take you from the basics, such as how to hold the knitting needles or crochet hook and create different types of stitches, to more advanced skills, such as how to add decorative touches to your projects and fix mistakes. The easy-to-follow information is communicated through clear, step-by-step instructions and accompanied by over 600 full-color photographs—perfect for any visual learner.

This book also includes numerous easy-to-follow patterns for all kinds of items, from simple crocheted scarves to cozy knitted baby outfits.

ISBN: 1-59200-862-3
Price: $24.99 US; $33.95 CDN
Page count: 304

WEIGHT TRAINING

MARAN ILLUSTRATED™ Weight Training is an information-packed guide that covers all the basics of weight training, as well as more advanced techniques and exercises.

MARAN ILLUSTRATED™ Weight Training contains more than 500 full-color photographs of exercises for every major muscle group, along with clear, step-by-step instructions for performing the exercises. Useful tips provide additional information and advice to help enhance your weight training experience.

MARAN ILLUSTRATED™ Weight Training provides all the information you need to start weight training or to refresh your technique if you have been weight training for some time.

ISBN: 1-59200-866-6

Price: $24.99 US; $33.95 CDN

Page count: 320

YOGA

MARAN ILLUSTRATED™ Yoga provides a wealth of simplified, easy-to-follow information about the increasingly popular practice of Yoga. This easy-to-use guide is a must for visual learners who prefer to see and do without having to read lengthy explanations.

Using clear, step-by-step instructions accompanied by over 500 full-color photographs, this book includes all the information you need to get started with yoga or to enhance your technique if you have already made yoga a part of your life. MARAN ILLUSTRATED™ Yoga shows you how to safely and effectively perform a variety of yoga poses at various skill levels, how to breathe more efficiently, how to customize your yoga practice to meet your needs and much more.

ISBN: 1-59200-868-2
Price: $24.99 US; $33.95 CDN
Page count: 320

Did you like this book? MARAN ILLUSTRATED™ offers books on the most popular computer topics, using the same easy-to-use format of this book. We always say that if you like one of our books, you'll love the rest of our books too!

Here's a list of some of our best-selling computer titles:

Guided Tour Series - 240 pages, Full Color

MARAN ILLUSTRATED's Guided Tour series features a friendly disk character that walks you through each task step by step. The full-color screen shots are larger than in any of our other series and are accompanied by clear, concise instructions.

	ISBN	Price
MARAN ILLUSTRATED™ Computers Guided Tour	1-59200-880-1	$24.99 US/$33.95 CDN
MARAN ILLUSTRATED™ Windows XP Guided Tour	1-59200-886-0	$24.99 US/$33.95 CDN

MARAN ILLUSTRATED™ Series - 320 pages, Full Color

This series covers 30% more content than our Guided Tour series. Learn new software fast using our step-by-step approach and easy-to-understand text. Learning programs has never been this easy!

	ISBN	Price
MARAN ILLUSTRATED™ Windows XP	1-59200-870-4	$24.99 US/$33.95 CDN
MARAN ILLUSTRATED™ Office 2003	1-59200-890-9	$29.99 US/$39.95 CDN
MARAN ILLUSTRATED™ Excel 2003	1-59200-876-3	$24.99 US/$33.95 CDN
MARAN ILLUSTRATED™ Access 2003	1-59200-872-0	$24.99 US/$33.95 CDN
MARAN ILLUSTRATED™ Computers	1-59200-874-7	$24.99 US/$33.95 CDN

101 Hot Tips Series - 240 pages, Full Color

Progress beyond the basics with MARAN ILLUSTRATED's 101 Hot Tips series. This series features 101 of the coolest shortcuts, tricks and tips that will help you work faster and easier.

	ISBN	Price
MARAN ILLUSTRATED™ Windows XP 101 Hot Tips	1-59200-882-8	$19.99 US/$26.95 CDN